W9-AKD-953

LADIES
FIRST

40 Daring American Women Who Were Second to None

ELIZABETH CODY KIMMEL

Foreword by Stacy Allison
First American Woman to Summit Mount Everest

NATIONAL
GEOGRAPHIC
WASHINGTON, D.C.

The type for this book is set in Whitman.

Printed in the United States of America

Library of Congress Cataloging-in-Publication Data

Kimmel, Elizabeth Cody.
Ladies first : 40 daring American women who were second to none / by Elizabeth Cody Kimmel.
    p. cm.
    ISBN 0-7922-5393-0 (trade edition) ISBN 0-7922-5394-9 (library edition)
1. Women—United States—Biography—Juvenile literature. 2. United States—Biography—Juvenile
literature. I. Title.
CT3260.K56 2005
920.72'0973—dc22   2005005113

Jacket/cover photos, clockwise from top left: Lynn Hill: Tony Duffy/Getty Images; Jane Addams: (c)
Bettmann/Corbis; Marian Anderson: (c) Bettmann/Corbis; Martha Graham: (c) Hulton-Deutsch
Collection/Corbis; Wilma Rudolph: (c) Bettmann/Corbis; Margaret Bourke-White: (c) Bettmann/Corbis;
Edna St. Vincent Millay: (c) Corbis

Interior photos: Pages 2, 14: James Schnepf; 2, 18: Courtesy of the Department of Historical Collections,
Health Sciences Library, SUNY Upstate Medical University; 2, 22: © Bettmann/Corbis; 2, 26: Molly
Bingham/World Picture Network; 2, 30: © Bettmann/Corbis; 2, 34: Chris Arend; 2, 38: © Bettmann/Corbis;
2, 42: A'Lelia Bundles/Walker Family Collection; 2, 46: © Bettmann/Corbis; 2, 50: © Bettmann/Corbis; 2,
54: Tony Duffy/Getty Images; 2, 58: Illustration by Mary O'Keefe Young from *Revolutionary Poet: A Story
of Phillis Wheatley*/Carolrhoda Books; 2, 62: Courtesy of Stacy Allison; 2, 66: © Bettmann/Corbis; 2, 70:
AP/Wide World Photos; 2, 74: © Bettmann/Corbis; 2, 78: © Bettmann/Corbis; 2, 82: Reginald Davis/Pix
Inc./Time Life Pictures/Getty Images; 2, 86: Library of Congress; 2, 90: Library of Congress; 2, 94: Courtesy
of Shirley Muldowney; 2, 98: Mark Costanzo; 2, 102: Julia Morgan Collection, Special Collections,
California Polytechnic State University; 2, 106: © Underwood & Underwood/Corbis; 2, 110: © Robert F.
Butts/Courtesy of Moment Point Press; 2, 114: Yousuf Karsh/Camera Press/Retna Ltd.; 2, 118: Courtesy of
Women In Military Service For America Memorial Foundation; 2, 122: Topical Press Agency/Getty Images;
2, 126: Photo by Steve J. Sherman, Courtesy of the Opera Orchestra of New York; 2, 130:
© Tim Wright/Corbis; 2, 134: © Corbis; 2, 138: Taro Yamasaki/Time Life Pictures/Getty Images; 2, 142:
Susan Watts/*New York Daily News*; 2, 146: © Corbis; 2, 150: Peter G. Veit; 2, 154: Oil painting by Marian
Anderson; 2, 158: © Corbis; 2, 162: © Hulton-Deutsch Collection/Corbis; 2, 166: © Doug Menuez/Corbis;
2, 170: © Hulton-Deutsch Collection/Corbis.

To

MARNIE HILLSLEY and **INGRID GOFF-MAIDOFF**
—women who create and inspire

TABLE OF
CONTENTS

FOREWORD

Ladies First is a celebration of achievement by American women. The women in this book are as diverse as our nation in their backgrounds, personalities, and accomplishments. Yet, they all have succeeded by creating their own paths and staying true to their dreams.

While our society places significant value on accomplishments that are firsts, I do not believe any of these women did what they did for the purpose of being first. They pursued their goals because they were deeply important to them. Somewhere deep inside they knew they could reach those goals. *Ladies First* offers a glimpse into the lives of women who created opportunities to make a difference for themselves and in the lives of others.

As you read these accounts, think what you can learn from these women. Did they select a goal and create the opportunity to succeed? How much was their success simply a result of good fortune? What was it about them that led to their achievements, and how can you apply those same qualities to your own life?

The stories in *Ladies First* demonstrate what can be accomplished with a vision and the ability to see beyond barriers. These daring women have opened doors for generations to come and inspire us all to expect just a little more of ourselves.

STACY ALLISON,
First American woman to summit Mount Everest

INTRODUCTION

When I first began to compile names and ideas for a book on women's "firsts" in America, the task was daunting. The last few centuries have seen a dazzling acceleration in the advancement of American women, and the acceptance and celebration of their achievements. From the arena of sports through the halls of medicine to the world of art and music, there are a growing number of women whose names top the lists of "firsts." How could I begin to choose which 40 to include? What would make the achievements of one woman worthy of writing about, when so many others just as extraordinary would remain unsung until another day? Several years after beginning this task, my work on this book is drawing to a close. Somehow, from the reams and reams of information and history I have read through, I have selected my 40 women and told their stories.

Other than having accomplished a significant American "first," what do these 40 women have in common? What is the thread that binds them together? As I reread each of their stories as I have told them, I find that the answer is entirely subjective. The connective thread is nothing more than me: my imagination, my hopes, and my dreams. Each of the individuals included in this book somehow sparked my imagination, both as a storyteller and as a woman. Each of these women left some kind of mark on me. Some of them remind me of aspects of myself. Some of them represent everything I aspire to be. These are women I would want to have as friends.

The photographs of some of these women, including Nellie Bly, Laura Ingalls Wilder, Jane Roberts, and Lynn Hill, adorn the cluttered walls of my office. These are people who have long been known to me and inspired me, and in writing this book I leaped at the chance to in-clude them as subjects.

Other subjects began in the still of my mind as a question. Who was the first woman rabbi in America? The first major female conductor? The first American woman up Everest? These questions sent me to reference books, works of history, or sometimes simply Google. Once I had a name, like Sally Priesand or Eve Queler or Stacy Allison, I began the hunt for their stories. Ultimately what had begun as a question in my mind became a biographical answer, a face put to a name. A story. If the story really spoke to me, really gave me pause, I knew it was one I had to include in this book.

And some women were those who had already sparked my interest, though I had never had the opportunity to study them closely. I collected biographies, scanned newspapers and magazines, and surfed the Internet to research these names. Did Georgia O'Keeffe have a "first?" Did Marian Anderson? Edna St. Vincent Millay? Sometimes the answer was no. But usually, with enough research, it was a yes.

The resulting collection of American women's firsts is a tapestry of courageous, tenacious, and intrepid individuals. Each story is a thread that is in some way moving and awe-inspiring. As a whole, these threads create a fabric of an entirely unique design—a design that will only become more beautiful as more women add their own threads in the future.

First woman to become Principal Chief of the Cherokee Nation

1945–

Wilma Mankiller was born in Oklahoma, one of 11 children of a Cherokee father and a mother of Dutch and Irish heritage. Her family was tightknit and loving, and though they were so poor she sometimes had to wear clothes made from old flour sacks, Mankiller was happy in the wooded countryside of her birth.

Eleven years later in 1956, everything changed. Over one hundred years earlier, the Cherokee people had been forcibly removed from their homes in the southeastern United States and marched to present-day Oklahoma over what is today called the Trail of Tears. Now the United States government was again pressing the Cherokee to relocate, not using force this time, but with promises of a better life elsewhere. Intrigued by the claim, Mankiller's father made the decision to participate in the government's plan to "mainstream" Cherokee families into large cities.

The family's new home would be San Francisco, California, and for Mankiller it was a bewildering and devastating change. It was not until she discovered the local San Francisco Indian Center that Mankiller found a place where she felt at home. As she progressed through school, Mankiller felt she had no clear sense of direction in her life. When her boyfriend proposed, seventeen-year-old Mankiller agreed to marry him. Within three years the couple had two daughters. But marriage and family did not change Mankiller's feeling of being out of place in California.

In October 1969, the eyes of the Native American community focused on the island of Alcatraz. Long used as a federal high-security prison, Alcatraz had been abandoned since 1963. Using the terms of an 1868 treaty that permitted Native Americans to file for a homestead on vacant federal property, a large group of activists landed on Alcatraz. On November 9, 1969, they took symbolic possession of the island "in the name of Indians of all tribes." For the next 19 months 89 people remained there, and were joined by others including Wilma Mankiller and four of her siblings. Much later in life, Mankiller would say that her journey began on Alcatraz. It was there, alongside fellow protesters working for the good of all Native Americans, that she finally experienced the sense of purpose she had longed for. Now Mankiller wanted to do more for her people.

> "I was raised in a household where no one ever said to me, 'You can't do this because you're a woman, Indian, or poor.' No one told me there were limitations. Of course, I would not have listened to them if they had tried."

By the mid-seventies Mankiller's marriage was failing, and she returned with her daughters to Oklahoma. She got a job with the Cherokee Nation of Oklahoma, helping members of her tribe get university educations, something she had obtained for herself in San Francisco. Mankiller soon proved herself an able fund-raiser and dedicated developer of programs, which got the attention of the Chief of the Cherokee Nation, Ross Swimmer. Mankiller knew she was appreciated, but she was very surprised when Chief Swimmer asked her to enter an election as his deputy Chief. No woman had ever held this position, and Mankiller encountered enormous resistance during the campaign by men who said she would make their tribe into a joke. She was openly threatened and her property vandalized. She received hate mail. It was exhausting, complicated by the fact that she was suffering from kidney disease and a degenerative illness called muscular dystrophy. The race was extremely close and resulted in a runoff between Mankiller and another candidate to decide the election. Mankiller won the 1983 election, becoming the first woman deputy Chief of the Cherokee Nation.

Opposition and lack of support continued to plague Mankiller during her next two years in office. She had to learn to work around the outright hostility of many council members. She felt frustrated and unwelcome. Times were still difficult in 1985, when Chief Swimmer accepted the leadership of the national Bureau of Indian Affairs from President Reagan. In accordance with the Cherokee Constitution, Mankiller automatically became Chief of the Cherokee Nation for the duration of Swimmer's term. Wilma Mankiller was now the first female chief of her people, although she had not been directly elected to the office.

When the time came for a new election in 1987, Mankiller agonized over whether to run for office. It would be considerably more difficult than her run for deputy Chief. The chances were not good that her people would elect her to be head of their tribe. And there were other factors to consider. She had remarried in 1986, to a Cherokee named Charlie Soap. The campaign would mean more time working and less time with her daughters and her new husband, and her health was not always good. Nevertheless she decided to run, embracing the Cherokee philosophy of becoming "of good mind," which meant embracing a wholly positive mindset and using setbacks as stepping stones. Mankiller won the election.

She was reelected for a second term in 1991 in a landslide victory. In 1995 when her term was completed, Mankiller decided it was time to step down from political life. She continues to live up to her name, which in Cherokee lore means a protector of the tribe, and at one time indicated military status similar to that of a captain. In living the tradition of her name, she has brought great honor to herself, her people, and to women everywhere.

First American woman to graduate from medical school

1821–1910

Who better to help a mother give birth than another mother? Since biblical times, women called midwives have specialized in working with women in childbirth. But in 1821, when Elizabeth Blackwell was born, upper-class women were turning more often to male doctors to deliver their babies. The attitude toward childbirth was changing, and birth was being seen more and more as a medical condition to be managed by a physician. And women were not permitted to become doctors.

Elizabeth Blackwell had personally witnessed the failure of medicine on several occasions. Four of her siblings died as infants. But the most significant loss was the death of her beloved father, Samuel Blackwell, a great thinker and an ardent supporter of social reform. After moving his family to America, he became sick. The "medicine" he was given to drink, sulfuric acid, only made his suffering more acute. It certainly did nothing to prevent his death, and might well have caused or at least hastened it.

Heartbroken, Blackwell took up teaching to help support her mother and siblings. In 1845, she met a young woman who was dying of uterine cancer. Because the uterus was central to reproduction and childbearing, it was considered an "improper" area of the body. It was therefore impossible for the woman to be adequately examined by a male physician. Before she died, the woman told Blackwell that her suffering would not have been as great if only a woman doctor could have treated her. She suggested that Blackwell should become a doctor herself. The idea of attempting to enter a field that was made up exclusively of men seemed ridiculous. Blackwell dismissed the idea out of hand. But it did not leave her mind altogether.

She was 24 years old and single, which in the eyes of the time labeled her an "old maid" and very unlikely ever to marry. She had a family that needed her to work and contribute financially, and a legacy from her father that anyone could and should try to change the world where it was needed. Blackwell decided to give medicine a try.

She applied to every medical school she could, but each one rejected her. When it seemed that every last door had firmly closed in her face, Blackwell received the surprising word that she had been accepted at the tiny Geneva Medical College of Western New York. In actuality, the board had put the vote to the student body (to avoid direct responsibility for rejecting Blackwell). The students, thinking the whole thing a prank, voted to admit Blackwell. When she actually appeared to begin her course of studies, they were forced to take her more seriously.

Blackwell found a mentor in the college's professor of anatomy, Dr. Webster. With his help, and recognizing her ambition and keen intellect, the students accepted Blackwell. By the time she graduated two years later, she was something of a heroine. But though she was now the first woman in America to obtain a medical degree, her hands were still effectively tied. No hospital in the country was going to employ a woman so she could obtain clinical experience. Blackwell would have to travel to Europe to get the hands-on experience necessary to become a working doctor.

She found that experience almost as hard to come by in Paris as it had been in New York. But in 1849 she finally found the opportunity at La Maternite, a hospital for midwives (who were still popular in France). During her stay there, she caught a contagious disease of the eye. Though she received every treatment available, the resulting infection caused Blackwell to lose the sight in that eye. She was bitterly disappointed that her partial blindness would prevent her from studying surgery. She went to England and worked at St. Bartholomew's hospital. Before returning to New York, she made friends with a young nurse named Florence Nightingale, who would eventually become world famous by revolutionizing nursing.

On her return to New York, Blackwell found it virtually impossible to get her practice started. However, by this time two more women had joined her cause. One was her younger sister, Emily Blackwell, who had followed her sister's path and obtained her own medical degree. The other was a German-speaking woman named Marie Zakrzewska who had been chief midwife at a hospital in Berlin. Together, the three women opened the country's first hospital staffed by women physicians: the New York Infirmary for Indigent Women and Children. It not only provided care for women by women but also provided free care to anyone who could not afford to pay.

"What chance have women, shut out from these instructions?"

With the coming of the Civil War, Blackwell organized a commission training nurses to help wounded soldiers, while continuing to run her infirmary. At the war's close, Blackwell realized yet another dream by founding a school for women physicians, the Women's Medical College of New York. She returned to her native England in 1869 to continue her pioneering work there, having fulfilled her dreams. As her father had encouraged, Blackwell found a system that was flawed, and changed it.

WILMA RUDOLPH

First American woman to win three gold medals
at a single Olympics

1940– 1994

By the age of four, the child who would become the fastest woman in the world was considered crippled for life. She had already exceeded expectations by surviving at all, having been born two months premature, weighing a fragile four and one half pounds. When she was four she was stricken with polio, a contagious disease that paralyzed and often killed children. When Rudolph recovered, she could not regain the use of her left leg. The doctor said she would never walk on the leg again. Rudolph's mother was not satisfied with the diagnosis. But there was not much in the way of quality medical care available to a black child with 21 brothers and sisters, whose parents made little more than $2,000 a year. It seemed nothing could be done. Wilma could never expect to lead even a normal life, let alone that of a world-class competitive athlete.

Those doors that illness had not closed to Rudolph, society had. Her hometown of Clarksville, Tennessee, was strictly segregated. Rudolph's mother could not change the racial bigotry of the community, but she could change her daughter's perception of her own health. Ignoring what the doctor had said, Mrs. Rudolph told her daughter that she would walk again, without a brace. She brought Rudolph 50 miles by bus twice each week to a medical college that provided physical therapy. With constant therapy, encouragement, and exhausting physical work, Rudolph proved her mother right. By the time she turned 12, Rudolph had stopped wearing her leg brace for good. For the first time in her life, she was completely healthy and strong.

Free from physical handicaps, Rudolph threw herself into athletics. Rudolph's startling abilities caught the attention of a college track coach, Ed Temple. He invited her to join a summer training program he was organizing for the most talented high school students in the area. Not only was it a great honor to be asked, it was also a chance for Rudolph to get a scholarship to college.

Speed and stamina came naturally to Rudolph, but more technical aspects of racing, such as pacing and strategy, had to be studied and learned. Temple taught her all she needed to know. A year later, with Temple's encouragement, Rudolph felt ready to try out for the 1956 Olympics. She made the cut, at 16 becoming the youngest woman on the U.S. women's Olympic track and field team.

Local Clarksville merchants generously gave Rudolph much of what she would need to travel to Australia to compete. The long journey to the greatest athletic competition in the world was tiring and unnerving, and Rudolph was disappointed in her performance. She was eliminated from the 200 meter dash in the semi-

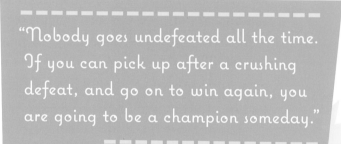

"Nobody goes undefeated all the time. If you can pick up after a crushing defeat, and go on to win again, you are going to be a champion someday."

final round. She did not go home empty-handed, however, as she won a bronze medal in the 400 meter relay. With four years to prepare for the next Olympics, Rudolph set her sights on the future.

In 1958, Rudolph enrolled at the University of Tennessee on a full athletic scholarship and got to work. When the Olympic trials came around in 1960, Rudolph easily qualified, and in what must have seemed an especially good omen, her own Coach Temple was made coach of the Olympic team. They traveled to Rome to prepare for the games. Rudolph's luck seemed to run out, however, when she twisted her ankle while training just days before her first big race.

She needn't have worried. Rudolph completed the 100 meter dash in an unbelievable 11 seconds, winning her first Olympic gold medal. Composed and unflappable, she repeated her performance in the 200 meter dash, winning the race and gaining her second gold. Suddenly, all eyes were upon her. If Rudolph and her teammates could win the 400 meter relay, Rudolph would take her third gold medal and make history in the process.

Amazingly, Rudolph's three teammates for the relay were also from Coach Temple's Tennessee State team. This meant they already had considerable experience running relay races together, a keen advantage. Rudolph fumbled the handoff of the baton from the runner before her. She almost dropped it, and took a moment to recover, losing the lead in the process. But in an incredible surge of speed and power, Rudolph passed the German leader and exploded across the finish line, winning the race and her third Olympic gold medal. She returned home a national hero, the fastest woman in the world. She appeared in newspapers, magazines, and on television. When a parade was held in her honor in her hometown, both black and white residents came out to cheer her. Wilma Rudolph, who was once told she would never walk, was elected Woman Athlete of the Year. To her great pride, she was invited to the White House to meet President Kennedy.

Two years before the 1964 Olympics, Rudolph decided to retire while still at the pinnacle of her success. Rudolph announced her retirement and her intention to serve as a goodwill ambassador and coach. She married, and continued her close involvement with athletic organizations like Operation Champ, which trained young inner city athletes. She later founded the Wilma Rudolph Foundation for aspiring young athletes.

In 1994, Rudolph was diagnosed with brain cancer and died several months later at the age of 54. Still young and active, the fastest woman in the world finally came to rest.

VICTORIA MURDEN

First woman to row across the Atlantic Ocean

1963–

At 8:46 a.m. on December 3, 1999, a 23-foot rowboat named *American Pearl* arrived at a dock in Pointe-a-Pitre, Guadeloupe. The lone rower, 36-year-old Victoria Murden, took her final stroke then shipped her oars and stood up. She stepped barefoot onto the dock to the sounds of cheering. She had just become the first woman, and the first American, to row solo across the Atlantic Ocean.

The Atlantic is the second largest of the world's oceans. On the route Murden chose to row, between the Canary Islands and Guadeloupe, the ocean stretched over three thousand miles. Murden's journey, which she undertook during the height of hurricane season, was her third attempt to row across the Atlantic Ocean. Many thought she must be out of her mind to try such a thing. But Murden was no stranger to challenge.

In 1988, she became the first woman to climb the Lewis Nunatak, a rocky peak jutting out of the glacial ice in Antarctica near the Thiel Mountains. In January 1989, on the same expedition, she skied to the geographic South Pole, something no American and no woman had ever done before. It was during those expeditions that she learned she could survive with just 30 pounds of gear and a well-planned food supply. In 1997, she entered a trans-Atlantic rowing race for two-person teams but was stricken with food poisoning just hours into the race. Her solo attempt to row across the Atlantic in 1998 ended when Murden encountered the battering winds of Hurricane Danielle. Her boat capsized 15 times before she could be rescued.

Having faced what seemed to be certain death, Murden was relieved to return home with a dislocated shoulder and a variety of cuts and bruises. However, her thoughts remained with her uncompleted journey, and when a company offered to sponsor her in another attempt less than a year later, she accepted.

Murden set out from the Canary Islands on September 13, a year to the day after returning to land when her last attempted crossing was cut short by the hurricane. Her boat, *American Pearl*, was packed with freeze-dried, high calorie meals, nuts, and snack bars. A desalinator would allow her to convert seawater to freshwater for drinking and the occasional bath. A small cabin provided enough room to sleep and take shelter in rough weather. Though she declined to take her sneakers because they added too much weight to the boat, she did pack a small selection of music and books on tape. The extra weight was made up for by the crucial help in fighting weeks of silence and boredom. With hard work and the best possible weather, she might make the crossing in just over two months. If the weather and wind did not cooperate, it could take significantly longer.

Murden spent the first day battling seasickness and frustration as the currents and wind pushed her back in the direction she'd come. After several days, however, her speed picked up, and she began to settle into a rhythm. Connected via satellite link to the Internet and with a working Iridium telephone, Murden could report her progress to friends and family, and could receive all-important weather updates. She was on her way. It was now a question of perseverance, strength, endurance, and luck. Plotting her position with the help of a GPS, or global positioning satellite,

> "If I choose not to live an 'every slice wrapped' kind of life, it is because so much of life lies outside the packaging."

Murden could calculate the distance she had come with precision. By October 18, she had reached the halfway point.

Week after week, and into months, she pushed on. Sometimes she was escorted by dolphins and whales, sometimes battered by thunderstorms, and occasionally she was entertained by swirls of tiny luminescent creatures stirred up in the water by her oars. Every day Murden rowed and slept, slept and rowed. By late November she was just four hundred miles from Guadeloupe. But the weather news was not good. Hurricane Lenny was now in the picture. Murden had hardly forgotten her near death experience with Hurricane Danielle the year before. She knew that rowing into another hurricane would most probably be the end of her voyage, and possibly the end of Murden altogether. But this time, fortune favored *American Pearl.* Though Lenny tossed Murden about, and even capsized her boat, she ultimately passed through the storm unharmed.

From her GPS she knew she was close, and when Murden caught sight of the Guadeloupe harbor, her journey was near its end. When she stepped ashore on the morning of December 3, a crowd of friends and supporters had gathered and stood cheering and blowing airhorns. Someone gave her a pair of sandals, since she had no shoes of her own to put on. A slew of television appearances and interviews awaited her. For those who had followed her progress daily on her website, and for those who had just learned about her accomplishment, Tori Murden was a hero. Safely on land, her goal accomplished, she was no longer asked "why," but "how." Her reply: "One of my teachers taught me the impossible just takes a little longer. And if you want to do something that is really important to you, surround yourself with honorable people, and it's really, really hard to fail. One stroke at a time, one step at a time, the impossible is easy to achieve."

MARGARET BOURKE-WHITE

First woman photographer to document active war combat missions

1904–
1971

One of the best known photographers of the 20th century, Margaret Bourke-White was willing to do anything to snap a great picture. A famous photograph of her in action shows her perched with her camera on a gargoyle high up on New York's Chrysler Building, jutting out some eight hundred feet over the street below. Margaret Bourke-White had not been raised to limit herself to what was safe, but rather to look fear straight in the face.

Born in New York in 1904, she was raised in a strict but intellectually rich household where her love of insects and reptiles was encouraged, and she was taught to conquer all her fears. While in college, Bourke-White became interested in photography and discovered she had a natural ability for it. Needing a source of outside income during her senior year, Bourke-White began snapping shots of campus buildings and soon found them selling briskly.

In 1929, the publisher Henry Luce hired the young photographer to shoot pictures for his new business and industry magazine, *Fortune*. She soon became one of the magazine's most important contributors, and when Luce began a new magazine called *Life*, which would feature photography, he immediately hired Bourke-White.

By the time she reached her early thirties, Bourke-White had documented a wide scope of the human experience. She had traveled to Russia to photograph factories and their workers. She had gone to the American Midwest to cover the devastation the 1934 drought had inflicted on the area described as the Dust Bowl.

31

Bourke-White teamed up with the writer Erskine Caldwell, whom she would later marry, to photograph sharecropping farmers and other struggling residents of the rural South.

By 1941, World War II had exploded in Europe, and *Life's* editor suspected that a German invasion of Russia was imminent. He asked Bourke-White if she wanted to go to Moscow, and she jumped at the chance. Bourke-White set up her cameras atop the bull's eye of Moscow's U.S. Embassy, photographing the storm of bombs and shells exploding all around her. She covered a total of 22 German bomb attacks on Moscow. When she returned home, the Army War College appointed her a U.S. Air Force photographer, and her position as a war correspondent was now official.

Though she begged the Army War College to send her to cover combat missions, the Air Force was reluctant to place a woman in such direct danger. Instead, they allowed her to join a fleet of ships carrying troops headed for North Africa to battle German forces stationed there. Five days of violent storms and 60-foot waves left everyone on board exhausted and on edge. But with constant drilling on procedure to abandon ship, they were prepared for disaster when it came.

The vessel was torpedoed by a German submarine in the black of night. Everyone was ordered to abandon ship. Bourke-White climbed into a lifeboat, not knowing if she would survive. All around her in the water floated pieces of wreckage and the forms of soldiers and nurses, some already drowned. Bourke-White and the others in her lifeboat could do nothing but hang on and wait, bailing water out of their boat with their helmets. A British boat rescued them the next day. She later wrote that a photographer's greatest pictures are the untaken ones, referring to the images she carried in her mind of that long dark night.

When she arrived in Africa, Bourke-White was still determined to join a combat mission. Given that she had already survived a German attack, the Air Force decided to give her permission to fly with a bomber. She joined the crew of a B-17 bomber called the *Flying Flit Gun* and flew with them for two weeks as they targeted a North African airfield. The photos ran in the next issue of *Life*, complete with a shot of Bourke-White in a leather flight-suit.

Bourke-White next traveled to Italy, to record the ground war between the Germans and Allied Forces, including British and American troops. When she finally returned home, she was greeted with news that devastated her. One of the two packages of film she had mailed had never arrived at the *Life* offices. Half of the photographs for which she had risked her life, including many of active combat, would never be seen by anyone.

> "Nothing attracts me like a closed door. I cannot let my camera rest until I have pried it open, and I wanted to be first."

Bourke-White continued to witness and document some of the most profound and tragic human experiences of her time. She was along with General Patton's Third Army in 1945 to photograph the liberation of the notorious death camp Buchenwald. After the war, she went to India and photographed Mohandas Gandhi, the legendary advocate of nonviolence and the spiritual leader of the Indian people. Her last visit with Gandhi took place mere hours before an assassin's bullet cut him down.

By the late fifties, Bourke-White began to suffer from the effects of a degenerative illness called Parkinson's disease. Though she held fast for years with physical therapy and surgery, the disease eventually claimed her life in 1971. She was only 67 years old.

In spite of her premature death, Bourke-White left a legacy of photographs and books that recorded, through her lens and her utterly unique spirit, the very worst and the very best that life has to offer.

SUSAN BUTCHER

1954–

The Iditarod is one of the toughest races in the world, and it takes place over some of the most challenging landscape on the planet. It is a race by dogsled that follows a route over a thousand miles long through the wilderness of Alaska. No woman has triumphed more consistently over this relentless challenge than Susan Butcher.

Born in Massachussetts in 1954, Butcher was drawn as a child to the wilderness and to the animals that filled it. Her parents were interested in boats and sailing, but Butcher seems to have been born with a passion for the outdoors not shared with family members. When she was eight, she wrote a two-sentence essay that read: "I hate the city. I love the country."

Two pet Siberian huskies kindled her interest in dogsled racing. Butcher had always known she would spend her life working in some way with animals. When she decided to move to Colorado at age 17 to become a professional dog musher, or driver, her parents were less than pleased. They would have preferred their daughter go to college. But Butcher had always been a child who knew what she wanted to do, and did it. She moved with her two huskies to Colorado in 1972. In her spare time she studied veterinary medicine at a nearby university, focusing on the care of dogs. In 1973, she heard about the first Iditarod Trail Sled Dog Race being organized in Alaska. Everything about Alaska, especially the pioneer-style living its wilderness offered, appealed to Butcher. In 1975, she found work at the University of Alaska and moved to Fairbanks. At the same time, she began to put together a team of dogs to enter in the Iditarod.

Training for the Iditarod encompasses a wide scope of activities. To begin with, both the musher of the dogsled and the entire team of dogs must be in top physical condition. Both Susan and her dogs trained up to 16 hours a day, seven days a week. They had to develop the physical stamina they would need to endure over two weeks of peak performance under challenging and sometimes dangerous conditions. Training to work with each other is also a crucial part of preparation for the Iditarod.

The musher must have faith in each and every dog on her team, and most important, she must have a lead dog whom she can trust with her life. A lead dog must be able to assert himself over the other dogs and make snap judgments on the trail if an obstacle suddenly looms into view. And a lead dog must be able to make decisions even if they go against what the musher is commanding. One of Butcher's lead dogs refused to turn left on a river path early on in the training. It was only after the dog pulled Butcher and the team in the opposite direction that the reason became clear. The portion of trail to the left was a flimsy snow bridge that would have collapsed under the weight of the team, send-

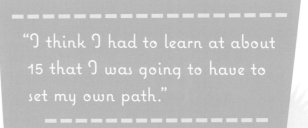

"I think I had to learn at about 15 that I was going to have to set my own path."

ing dogs, sled, and musher into the river. The lead dog's instinct had been absolutely correct. To cultivate and recognize this instinct, Butcher bonded with her dogs and treated them as friends, family, and professional athletes. In her earliest years training for the Iditarod, Butcher explains that living in the wilderness to train, the dogs were not just friends to her, they were her only friends at all.

By the time Butcher was ready to enter her first Iditarod in 1978, the race was still largely the domain of men. Only three women had previously completed the course. Butcher was not welcomed with open arms, but she chose to ignore the resistance from the male mushers. She finished the race in 19th place, which was an extremely respectable showing for a newcomer, man or woman, and made her the first woman to place in the top 20.

Butcher ran the Iditarod every year after that, and by 1984 she had placed second in two races. She now felt she was good enough to win the Iditirod outright, but in 1985 her dreams were cut violently short. Early on in the race she and her team came upon a pregnant and hungry moose, which charged the dogs, attacking them with its massive hooves. Two of Butcher's dogs were killed, and many others badly hurt. Butcher chose to withdraw from the race to tend to her dogs' injuries, leaving another woman, Libby Riddles, to become the first woman to win the Iditarod.

In 1986, it was Butcher's turn. Though two of her dogs fell through the ice while they were leading the sled over a river, Butcher was able to pull the dogs to safety and continue the race. Sleeping only a few hours each night, she overtook other teams one at a time, until she had taken the lead. Eleven days after starting, Butcher and her team crossed the finish line in first place. She had not only won the race, she had also set a new speed record. Nine years after running her first Iditarod as a "rookie," Susan Butcher had now earned the respect and admiration of almost every other musher, male and female alike.

She repeated her feat in 1987, winning the race again and beating her own speed record in the process. In 1988, Butcher took first place yet again, becoming the first musher ever to win the race three consecutive times. Her accomplishments made her arguably the best musher ever to race, and her reputation in the world of athletes was now legendary.

Butcher continued to race the Iditarod every year through 1994, winning the race one additional time, and always placing in the top ten. Butcher now raises Alaskan Huskies at her Trail Breaker Kennels, and her achievements are still among the very greatest of the Iditarod.

JANE ADDAMS

First American woman to win the
Nobel Peace Prize

1860–1935

Born into a well-to-do family in Cedarville, Illinois, Jane Addams was well provided for financially in her childhood. However, she was deeply affected by several losses, beginning with the death of her beloved mother when Addams was only two years old. Four years later her sister Martha died of typhoid fever. Addams herself was sickly and suffered damage to her spinal cord after an illness. Even as a child, Addams realized that her privileged upbringing could not protect her from the hazards of disease and accidents that made the death of children or their parents all too common.

Addams was determined to educate herself during a time when it was still unusual for a woman to pursue higher education. She received what today we could consider a college degree from Rockford Female Seminary in 1881 and planned to enroll in medical school. However, Addams, who always suffered back pain and seemed to frequently catch viruses, developed a lingering illness after her Rockford graduation. The exact nature of her illness is not known, and there may have been some degree of mental exhaustion or depression involved. Whatever she had weakened her to the point that she gave up her plans to pursue a medical degree. Her father and stepmother, neither of whom felt a woman should pursue a man's career, may also have worked to convince her to remain at home with them.

In 1887, Addams took a trip to Europe. After visiting a university community house called Toynbee Hall in London, an idea began to take shape. Toynbee Hall had been created to give Oxford and Cambridge students a place to live while working on behalf of the poor, and was called a "settlement house." The primary purpose of the settlement house was to enable students to live together in a very poor section of town, to help the underprivileged.

> "I do not believe that women are better than men. We have not wrecked railroads, nor corrupted legislature, nor done many unholy things that men have done; but then we must remember that we have not had the chance."

With her friend Ellen Starr, Addams returned to the United States and founded a settlement house of her own in Chicago. She acquired space in an abandoned mansion located in the heart of the immigrant section of the city. Later known as Hull House, the settlement provided free classes and programs for the local poor and served as a gathering place for intellectuals, social reformers, and free thinkers. Kindergarten and child-care were also available. Addams and Starr both lived in Hull House themselves.

Addams next began to address issues that caused poverty or forced the poor to remain poor. She worked on behalf of low-wage workers, particularly children, and her work was instrumental in the formation of new laws to prohibit abuses in the workplace. She also worked to help women win the right to vote, or suffrage.

Her work for voting rights resulted in her election to the National American Women Suffrage Association. This was only one of a number of influential groups with which Addams was involved. She was instrumental in forming groups as well, including two that remain extremely powerful and influential to this day. One is the American Civil Liberties Union (ACLU), an organization that works to protect the individual's right to freedom. The second is the National Association for the Advancement of Colored People

(NAACP), an organization that works to protect the civil rights of black Americans.

In 1912, Addams campaigned on behalf of former president Theodore Roosevelt and the Progressive Party, a movement that embraced many of the social and industrial reform issues nearest to Addams's heart. At this time in her life, Addams enjoyed almost universal popularity, acclaim, and celebrity.

Ironically, it was pacifism, or peacekeeping efforts, that caused her reputation to suffer serious damage. Addams and many of her friends opposed war in any form. In 1914, war erupted in Europe, and Addams opposed America's entering what would eventually be called the First World War. She helped to form the Women's Peace Party and to launch an international effort by women to organize the movement for peace. Though she would later win the Nobel Peace Prize for her work, some of the public began to turn against her. When she returned to the United States, she found many of her previous supporters speaking out against her pacifist efforts. The most notable objector was Theodore Roosevelt, who called Addams and other activist women "hysterical pacifists." Many who withdrew their support felt that patriotism and support of the government were crucial and that it was an inappropriate time to suggest peace at any cost.

Addams continued her work by opposing strict immigration laws and pushing for the regulation of businesses. By 1930, Addams had reclaimed the respect of the public and was the recipient of many honorary degrees and awards. None was so important to her as the Nobel Peace Prize, which she was awarded in 1931. She was the first American woman to receive this honor.

By the time of her death in 1935, Addams was once again recognized internationally as one of the most influential social reformers in America. Thousands attended her funeral, and in the decades since she has remained among the very highest ranks of American women for her vision, her dedication, and her accomplishments.

MADAM C. J. WALKER

First female African American self-made millionaire

1867–1919

It was perhaps one of the longest and most improbable journeys of her time. From the cotton fields of Louisiana, a child then called Sarah Breedlove cast her gaze beyond her family's one-room cabin and dreamed of something better for herself. She was born in 1867 to recently freed slaves, was orphaned by seven, married at 14, and widowed by 20. With a child to raise, Breedlove chose to leave Louisiana, and moved with her daughter to St. Louis, Missouri, where she soon found work as a washerwoman. Washing clothes was exhausting and paid very little. As her daughter, Lelia, blossomed in her 16th year, Breedlove began to wonder if her daughter's future would hold nothing more fulfilling than a lifetime of scrubbing dirty linens.

Breedlove's greatest opportunity began as a pesky problem. Due to a combination of factors probably including poor diet, high stress, and improper care, she began to suffer from scalp problems that caused some of her hair to fall out. After much searching, she found a product that seemed to help. She not only used the ointment herself, but also began to act as a sales agent for its inventor, Annie Malone.

Breedlove began experimenting with her own recipe for a hair and scalp treatment for African American women, finally hitting on a key combination of ingredients that she later said came to her in a dream. Breedlove began producing and selling her new product on her own. She married C. J. Walker in 1906 and the family settled in the growing city of Denver, Colorado. There, she began an aggressive door-to-door campaign as Madam C. J. Walker. In addition to selling

"Madam Walker's Wonderful Hair Grower," she offered a course of instruction in scalp treatment and hair growing, for which there seemed to be an ever-growing supply of students. She also began selling her products by mail order.

Within several months, Walker's business had exploded and she was making almost $70 a week, more than ten times her weekly earnings as a washerwoman. The response to both her products and her classes continued to be overwhelming. By 1908, Walker established the first headquarters for her business in Pittsburgh, Pennsylvania. Two years later, she transferred her operations to Indianapolis, where she purchased a large home and began building the first Madam C. J. Walker factory.

What might have remained simply a highly profitable business began to grow into something even more significant. As her wealth and influence grew, Madam Walker increasingly used her power and money to help others. In her mind, strengthening her business meant the opportunity to increase her charitable work, so she sought membership in Booker T. Washington's influential National Negro Business League. At first she was denied membership, as Washington felt that her cosmetic products were supporting the imitation of white standards of beauty by black women. When Walker finally met with Washington, she was able to convince him of both the significance of her business and her personal commitment to philanthropy, or giving to charitable causes.

At the height of her success, Walker had developed a profound desire to contribute to the advancement of the black American. Her work included not just marketing her products but also lecturing on the growth of her own business to provide proof to her peers that an African American man or woman could achieve extraordinary

> "I got my start by giving myself a start."

financial and professional success. She became perhaps the most significant female African American philanthropist of her time.

Madam C. J. Walker was now providing unprecedented job opportunities for thousands, mostly black, women. In addition to employees involved in the making and distribution of her products, Madam Walker had a growing number of sales agents. They received a generous salary to sell Walker products door-to-door and hold demonstrations and classes to teach the Walker method for scalp treatment and hair growing and straightening. The little girl who had begun life in the poverty-stricken fields of Louisiana provided women with the means to improve their appearance and also with the opportunity to pursue a promising career. To women and black Americans in general, she was living proof that the avenues to wealth were not closed to anyone. And through her constant donations, scholarships, and work on behalf of charities, she literally shared her wealth with those in need.

Madam Walker's generosity and sense of civic responsibility were incorporated into her business, and her own employees and sales agents were always encouraged to follow her example. By the time Madam Walker moved to New York City in 1914, she was in the circle of the most influential and important civic and cultural leaders, black and white, of her day.

It is impossible to know the precise amount of her fortune at the time of her death in 1919. Newspapers widely reported the amount as exceeding one million dollars, and her own lawyer named her as the first African American self-made millionaire. In her biography, Walker's great-great-granddaughter suggests the amount may have been less. Regardless, Madam C. J. Walker was certainly the wealthiest, most driven and accomplished African-American woman of her time, and ambitious to her very final hour. Her last words are reported to have been "I want to live to help my race."

1864–1922

What hadn't Nellie Bly done to make headlines? On any given day she was as famous a news item as she was a reporter—one of the first women in the country to break into the all-male ranks of the newspaper world. Ever since her very first New York assignment—posing as a lunatic to uncover the terrifying conditions of the state mental asylum—she had forged fearlessly ahead with her reporting.

Nellie Bly was born Elizabeth Cochran in Pennsylvania, in 1864. Her family was large and wealthy, and she spent her childhood in a luxurious home. But her life changed suddenly when her beloved father died just after her sixth birthday. The family's beautiful home had to be sold, and money for the large family was in short supply. When she was old enough, she enrolled in a teacher's college but could not afford to complete the program. With no money and the prospect of making a living as a teacher suddenly gone, Elizabeth Cochran's future was uncertain. She did not want to marry, so she had to find some way to make a living. She moved to Pittsburgh with two of her brothers and wrote a column on the theater for the paper.

Soon she grew bored. Wanting to write more serious articles, she headed to a city known for its newspapers—New York. With great perseverance, she got into the office of the editor of the *New York World*, John Cockerill. He scoffed at the idea of hiring a woman reporter, until she offered to prove herself through an outrageous and dangerous stunt. Cochran proposed to pose as an insane woman, have herself committed to an insane asylum, then write an article about the experience. Unable to resist, the editor agreed. The resulting story, written under the name Nellie Bly not only grabbed the attention of New York City, it spawned a movement to improve appalling conditions in insane asylums. John Cockerill had his hit story, and Nellie Bly had a new job as a full-time reporter with the *New York World*.

Now Bly was pitching a new, equally outrageous idea to Cockerill. Like countless others, she had read Jules Verne's *Around the World in Eighty Days*, inspired by Verne's imagination of breaking the record for traveling around the world. If Verne's fictional character could set a new world record, why should Bly herself not be the first to break it?

International travelers of the time had few modes of transportation to choose from, and conditions were unpredictable, slow, and sometimes dangerous. She packed extremely lightly. She had a traveling dress made especially to last through 80 days of daily wear. Everything else, including toiletries and several changes of underclothes, was crammed into one tiny suitcase. Bly meant to travel light, and she meant to travel fast.

In Hoboken, New Jersey, she boarded the steamer *Augusta Victoria* bound for England. She spent the first day at the railing on deck, throwing up, but soon grew accustomed to the roll of the ship. Arriving in England seven and a half days later, she crossed the English Channel by ferry and took a train to the French city of Amiens, where she devoted a precious hour to meeting Jules Verne himself, a great enthusiast of her journey. With his blessing and friendship, she pressed on.

"Energy rightly applied and directed will accomplish anything."

By train to Italy. By steamer to Egypt, modern day Yemen, Sri Lanka, and Singapore, where she acquired a pet monkey. Again by boat, to Hong Kong, where she learned a rival newspaper had sent a woman named Elizabeth Brisland around the world in the opposite direction, to beat Bly's time.

Bly boarded the liner *Oceanic*, a ship known just as much for its speed as for its luxury, en route to San Francisco. In spite of encountering a terrible storm, *Oceanic* arrived in San Francisco on January 20 in good time. Nellie Bly had come 21,000 miles in 68 days.

In a four-and-a-half-day relay race of train connections, Bly crossed the country and arrived in New Jersey on January 25, 72 days after leaving. She had broken every record for circling the globe and beaten Elisabeth Bisland. Readers across the country had followed Bly's progress in newspapers, and huge crowds waited to greet her on her arrival in New Jersey. Sales of the *World* increased dramatically. It would be a difficult feat to follow.

Bly may never have reached the heights of her globe-trotting celebrity again, but she continued to work as a dedicated reporter. She covered the violent Pullman train worker's strike in 1894, and the movement to gain women the vote. During World War I she became the first woman reporter to visit the war's eastern front. In later years she spent much of her time writing about and working on behalf of orphaned children.

Bly died in 1922 of pneumonia, at the age of 57. She was considered one of the best reporters in the country, still most famous for her trip around the world. Nellie Bly had proved that sometimes, coming home is the greatest accomplishment of all.

EMMA HART WILLARD

Established first higher education institution for women

1787–1870

In 1787, Emma Hart was born the 16th of the 17 children of Samuel and Lydia Hinsdale Hart in Berlin, Connecticut. A girl of this era might expect to receive an extremely limited education, including only enough reading skills to permit her to read her Bible, and perhaps develop artistic or musical abilities. In fact it was widely believed that females were incapable of absorbing more sophisticated learning, and that attempting to instruct them might actually damage their health.

In spite of the extremely limited intellectual expectations society had of women, Emma Hart's father nonetheless encouraged his daughter to read, seek out education, and exercise her mind. Though traditional schooling was not available to her, she was encouraged to pursue her own education by any means she could find. This encouragement and freedom given by her father instilled in Emma Hart a lifelong love of learning. In this era teaching was one of the only professions considered acceptable for an unmarried woman. By the age of 20 she was an experienced teacher, having taught in the local Berlin Academy and several other schools nearby. When she met her future husband, Dr. John Willard, she was the head of an academy in Middlebury, Vermont.

Under other circumstances, Hart's marriage to Dr. Willard might have seen the end of her teaching career altogether. Married women were not expected to work but rather to devote themselves full time to their home and family. However, two years after the birth of their son John, the Willards suffered a serious financial loss related to

Willard's business. To increase their income, Emma Willard began teaching girls in her home, calling the institution the Middlebury Female Seminary. The experience was proof to Willard that young woman were capable of significant academic achievements. Desiring to bring the most modern and complete teaching methods to her girls, Willard asked if she could sit in on the boy's examinations at Middlebury College, so that she could learn exactly what level of scholarship was expected of college-level students. Her request was refused. In spite of this setback, Willard felt confident enough in the abilities of her Middlebury students to begin writing her *Plan for Improving Female Education.*

The elegantly written pamphlet had a quiet tone and a well-organized, rational argument that concealed what was actually a revolutionary proposal. Her "plan" suggested that the entire system of female education should be reformed and that state legislation should in part pay for a female seminary that would be similar to the college preparatory institutions that boys had. She discussed the defects of the current system for girls and shrewdly suggested that improving the way in which women are educated would in fact give the government more control of the character of their future male citizens—by improving the character of their mothers!

In reading the *Plan*, it is clear that however passionately Emma Willard wished to rebuild women's education, she was not suggesting radical change in social thinking. Willard carefully placed reassurances throughout her Plan emphasizing that she did not wish to move women into the sphere of men at that time. Her proposed areas of study, religious and moral; literary; domestic; and ornamental, were not threatening to men suspicious of women who wanted to expand their worlds beyond the limits of home. Willard sent her *Plan* to the governor of New York, DeWitt Clinton. A great supporter of education, Clinton found himself genuinely persuaded by her proposal. Governor Clinton put the plan before the state legislature, but they refused to approve the money to fund the institution.

Undeterred, Emma Willard continued in her campaign to establish a school for the higher education of girls. She printed and self-published her *Plan*, receiving letters of support from John Adams and Thomas Jefferson. Her efforts were ultimately rewarded. In 1820, the citizens of Troy, New York, had become convinced of the advantages of having an exceptional school for women established locally. They contacted Willard and offered to provide a building and raise funds if she would establish in Troy the "female seminary" she had described. She did not need to be asked twice, and in 1821 the Troy Female Seminary opened its doors, making history in the process.

The school was an immediate success, and it paved the way for the establishment of similar seminaries and ultimately for women's colleges such as Mount Holyoke. Renamed the Emma Willard School, the seminary became a model for the education of women and almost two hundred years later is still a vital and successful school for girls.

Emma Willard was not a firebrand. But by establishing the first higher education institution for women, she created a generation of women who placed great importance on educating their own daughters. The school graduated women who would ultimately contribute greatly to women's rights in America. With the acceptable standards of women's education effectively changed, the door was now open to future groundbreakers and further progress in the field. Emma Willard in her quiet, calculated manner helped pave the way for all the advancements women would win for generations to come.

> "Though well to decorate the blossom, it is far better to prepare for the harvest."

LYNN HILL

1961–

It was considered one of the last unconquered prizes in American rock climbing. El Capitan is a 3,000-foot high wall of granite in Yosemite Valley. The route up its face known as the Nose had been ascended by rock climbers from all over the world. But in 1993 no one had ever free-climbed the Nose. In the language of climbers, to "free" a route means to climb it using only one's hands and feet on the rocks. Ropes and protective gear are placed only to safeguard the climber in the event of a fall. So unlike the many other climbers who ascended the Nose with the help of climbing ropes and other equipment, Lynn Hill meant to reach the top using only her muscle and her will.

She was already considered one of the nation's greatest rock climbers, and has been called one of the best female athletes in the world. Small and powerfully lean with a gymnast's flexibility, Lynn Hill's career had included several firsts and many competition wins. She had also survived a catastrophic fall.

Lynn Hill was born in Detroit, Michigan, in 1961, and moved with her parents and six siblings to southern California when she was still a young child. There Hill turned to the outdoors for amusement. At a very young age she displayed a talent for climbing everything from monkey bars to the neighborhood light pole. When she was 14, she tagged along with her older sister to a local climbing slab and decided to have a try. She reached the top of the climb without faltering, aching but exhilirated. From that time on, first as a hobby and later as a profession, Hill climbed as often and as hard as she could.

The Nose is one of the most challenging and popular climbs in the country. Many dream of free-climbing it. In the years prior to Hill's attempt, all the climbers who tried ultimately failed. In the late summer of 1993, Hill was ready to give it a try herself. On her first attempt, it took Hill and her partner on the route, Simon Nadin, two days to ascend the first 2,000 feet. Each day had involved some 18 consecutive hours of climbing, followed by a few hours of exhausted sleep in bivouacs, or temporary camps, anchored on narrow rock ledges. By the morning of the third day, the most difficult work lay directly overhead. The heart-shaped Great Roof of El Capitan jutted out from the rock face, with only a thin crack leading straight up its center providing a place to hold on. The Great Roof had foiled every climber previously attempting to free-climb it. But here Hill's slight stature and slender hands would give her an advantage that her larger male counterparts did not have.

After watching her partner fail to get past the Great Roof, Hill worked her way upward, and found she could just barely get her fingers into the crack. As she moved up the lower part of the crack, her right foot slipped, and seconds later she hung from her safety rope. Undeterred, she began to reclimb the crack. This time, she inched past the spot where she had fallen and pulled herself up into a standing position on a ledge. She had just become the first person to free-climb the Great Roof.

There was one section left to climb, however. This next part of the Nose route, known as Changing Corners, defeated the exhausted climber. Neither Hill nor her partner could find a way up. Losing strength and daylight fast, they decided to abandon their attempt to free climb the Nose. But little more than a week later, Hill was back with another climber, Brooke Sandahl, who was himself interested in attempting the free-climb.

Hill had made it past the Great Roof once, so she knew she could do as much again. For several days, she focused her efforts on the section, or pitch, of the climb called Changing Corners. She and her partner hiked to the top of El Capitan and descended on ropes to Changing Corners, the pitch that had previously stopped her. For three days she worked tirelessly on the rock face trying different moves. When she could do no more, she and Sandhal hiked down to the ground and prepared to begin their free-climb attempt of the entire route from the valley floor to the summit.

They reached the Great Roof without incident, and Hill successfully free-climbed past it on her first try. Then, after a good night's sleep on a ledge just above the Great Roof, Hill was ready to take on the Changing Corners. As Sandhal watched in amazement, Hill bent and contorted her body like a Chinese acrobat. With subtle twists and using every inch of her body to exert pressure on the rock face, Hill seemed to flow upward. Moments later, without fanfare, she reached the top of the section. Though there were several pitches left to climb before the summit, Hill knew she had passed the only section that posed a serious obstacle to her. Though her partner was unable to duplicate her feat, they celebrated her victory together exuberantly at the summit. It was a highly symbolic moment, as Lynn Hill stood on the top of El Capitan with the world at her feet.

> "Imagination is key."

When she "freed" the Nose in her now legendary four-day effort, Lynn Hill stunned the climbing world. She returned a year later and created an amazing new record—replicating her free-climb in an unbelievable 23 hours. She was now not only the first person to free the Nose, she had also returned to set a speed record for the free-climb that boggled the mind of even the most grizzled climber. In her memoirs, Hill wrote that it took her years to fully digest what she did on that day. As of this writing, no climber, man or woman, has duplicated the climb.

PHILLIS WHEATLEY

First African American woman writer to be published

c.1753–1784

The exact year and village of her birth, even the name her mother gave her, are unknown. She crossed the ocean in the belly of a slave ship, and at the time of her arrival in Boston in 1761 she was a frail, trembling seven-year-old who spoke not one word of English. As was often the custom, she was given the surname of the man who purchased her, Wheatley. The Wheatleys did not have to look far for a first name. There, still in the harbor, was the slave ship that had transported the girl. Its name was the *Phillis*. The girl would carry the name of the ship with her all her life, as Phillis Wheatley.

The Wheatleys were a prosperous and respected Boston family. John Wheatley was a merchant and tailor. His wife, Susanna Wheatley, wished to add a domestic servant to her household to help care for her in later years. As Mrs. Wheatley's intended personal companion, the little girl was not responsible for the domestic tasks that the other household servants performed. She spent her time with Mrs. Wheatley, and it became readily apparent that the little African girl had an extraordinarily keen mind.

In just over a year, Phillis Wheatley was fluent in English and could read without error. She soon learned Latin, began studying geography and the classics, and began to read poetry. Her tutor was most likely one of the Wheatley's twin children, 18-year-old Mary and Nathaniel. It is not known when Wheatley began to display her remarkable gift for writing, but her first known letter was written to a minister when she was about 12 years old. It was probably around this time that she began to write poetry.

Wheatley was strongly encouraged in her studies by Mrs. Wheatley, and she achieved a level of education and intellectual accomplishment that was highly unusual for any girl of that period, let alone an African slave denied the most basic legal and social rights. Mrs. Wheatley encouraged the young poet to correspond with influential figures and often arranged for visits with important people who might later become Wheatley's patrons, influential supporters of an artist. By 1767, Mrs. Wheatley managed to get one of the poems published in a newspaper. Wheatley's fame increased. In 1770, she wrote an elegy, or a poem expressing sorrow for a death, for the Countess of Huntingdon when her chaplain, George Whitefield, died. Wheatley had heard him preach in Massachusetts, and Mrs. Wheatley knew and corresponded with the countess. Wheatley's poem greatly moved the countess, a powerful and influential London widow. Wheatley had found her patron.

> "But how, presumptuous shall we hope to find Divine acceptance with th'Almighty mind— While yet (O deed ungenerous!) they disgrace And hold in bondage Afric's blameless race?"

Mrs. Wheatley now sought to find a publisher for Wheatley's collection of poems. Though she spared no effort, she was unable to find one. Undaunted, Mrs. Wheatley turned her attention to England's publishers. She found a willing publisher in Archibald Bell, with one condition—she must provide proof that it was indeed an African girl who had written the poems. Some of the Wheatley's influential Boston friends provided a signed testament declaring the identity of the poet as truthful, and Wheatley was on her way to becoming published.

Now all that remained was to unite Wheatley with her patron and her British readers. In 1773, Wheatley boarded a ship en route to London, accompanied by Nathaniel Wheatley. Wheatley remained in London for six weeks, where she was treated as a celebrity. Unfortunately, her visit had to be cut short when Mrs. Wheatley became ill, and Wheatley returned to Boston to help care for her, without ever having the chance to meet Countess Huntingdon. It must have been disappointing to go home without having met her patron. However, the blow was softened by the news that the Wheatleys were granting the young poet her freedom, releasing her from slavery.

The effect of the publication of Wheatley's poems was vast. In addition to the prestige and celebrity it brought her, it also proved valuable ammunition for abolitionists and all opponents of slavery. It had long been claimed that Africans were destined to be slaves as they were incapable of the very simplest learning. The elegant and sophisticated poetry of Phillis Wheatley disproved the notion that Africans could not become every bit as educated as whites. Some of the most famous figures of the time, including John Hancock, Benjamin Franklin, and George Washington, counted themselves among Wheatley's admirers and supporters. With such influential witnesses to her authenticity, it was impossible for anyone to claim her published work as a hoax.

Wheatley's fortunes as a free woman eventually failed. Boston and the rest of the American colonies became embroiled in their war for independence from the British crown. Mr. and Mrs. Wheatley both died, and Wheatley found she could not support herself through her poetry and sewing. When she died in her early 30s, she was relatively impoverished and had little in the way of possessions.

But two hundred years later, the poems of Phillis Wheatley are still being read.

STACY ALLISON

First American woman to summit Mount Everest

1958–

On Nepal, its name can be translated as Goddess of the Sky. Called Mount Everest by many Westerners, it is the highest mountain in the world, towering more than 29,000 feet over Nepal and Tibet. It remained unclimbed until 1953, when Sir Edmund Hillary and Tenzing Norgay became the first ever to stand on its summit. Thirty-five years later, an American woman, Stacy Allison, would have her turn at the top.

Her family might have suspected climbing lay in Allison's future when she scaled a Douglas fir at a picnic when she was seven years old. Allison took up the sport of climbing seriously while in college, taking on the rock in Zion, Utah, ascending a route called Angel's Landing. In Zion, Allison met Scott Fischer, who would become a highly renowned mountain climber.

In addition to rock climbing, Allison began climbing mountains. Her first summit was the 300-foot peak of Mount Washington in the Cascade Range. Following that accomplishment, Allison took on progressively bigger and tougher mountains.

By 1987, Allison had proved herself as a mountaineer, having summited Denali in Alaska, which is North America's highest peak, and the Himalayas' Ama Dablam. When she approached Scott Fischer about joining his Everest expedition, he readily accepted her. It took the team weeks to lay the equipment and protection up the route they had chosen on the mountain's north face, and to lug gear and supplies to stock their camps. When Fischer included her in the first group that would try to reach the summit, Allison was in position to become the first American woman to stand on top of the world. But it was not to be. They had climbed past 23,500 feet when a sudden storm forced the summit team to take shelter in a snow cave. They hunkered down to wait it out, and after five days were able to climb up to 25,000 feet before it became clear that the vicious windstorm on the summit made proceeding impossible. Allison's opportunity was gone.

The following year, she won a spot on another expedition bound for Everest, though Scott Fischer was unable to secure himself a place. There were three women, including Allison, on the team.

The now familiar work of laying the gear up the ascent route and setting up the camps went without incident. Early on in the climbing, the combined American and Korean teams found themselves in the path of a roaring avalanche. The death rate on this section of Everest, called the Khumbu Icefall, is particularly high primarily due to avalanches. There was nowhere to take cover. The avalanche spluttered to a stop just one hundred feet away, and they continued climbing.

The team leader now decided on the first summit team—it would include himself, another male climber named Steve Ruoss, a Nepalese Sherpa named Pasang, and Stacy Allison. Two more Sherpas would climb with them, carrying the oxygen tanks until they were needed. But first, with all the gear now laid for their ascent, they returned to Base Camp to regather their strength.

"Everest is behind me now, but I can still see the shadow of the mountain in everything I do. It's a reminder, a challenge, from the highest spot in the world. Look beyond the ordinary. There's always something more. As long as I remember that, I know anything is possible."

Several days later they set out, Allison trudging across the snowy glacier in her warmest down and polyproylene layers. At Camp 2 they slept, climbing hard the following day and overnighting at Camp 3. They reached their final camp, two tents at 26,200 feet, and settled down to rest for the push to the summit the next morning.

The human body is not designed to survive at this excessive altitude. Generally, a climber who has access to food and water would be able to survive only about a week over 26,000 feet, which is why this altitude is known as "The Death Zone." Once there, a climber has a limited time to attempt the summit before being forced to descend or suffer from altitude sickness. The summit team was climbing hard and well but was suddenly faced with an unpleasant surprise. The two Sherpas climbing just below with their oxygen had inexplicably turned and begun their descent. They were too far gone to be stopped, and they had taken the crucial canisters of oxygen, which most climbers require as they approach the summit.

There was only enough oxygen left for one climber to reach the summit along with Pasang. Pasang thought of a number between one and ten, and each climber took a guess. The winner was Allison. She and Pasang would continue with their only oxygen toward the summit—alone.

They made their way up the ridge toward the summit, then up the cliff called the Hillary Step, then over the last precarious tightrope of ridge to the summit. Allison concentrated on walking cautiously and steadily until she reached the end of her climb. Standing on the summit of Mount Everest, Stacy Allison could literally go no higher.

Allison returned to America a celebrity. Everest remained behind, continuing to attract the strong of heart. In 1996, during one of the deadliest climbing seasons ever experienced on Everest, a total of 15 climbers died, including Allison's old friend Scott Fischer. Allison now writes and appears as a motivational speaker, living evidence of real accomplishment.

MARIAN ANDERSON

1897–1993

O n first hearing her sing, the legendary conductor Toscanini exclaimed, "A voice like yours is heard once in a hundred years." After hearing a recording of Anderson for the first time, the world famous singer Jessye Norman said, "I listened, thinking, 'This can't be just a voice, so rich and beautiful.' It was a revelation. And I wept." The entrenched racial prejudices and restrictions in the classical music world had seemed unmovable, but in Marian Anderson's voice there was a force powerful enough to shake them.

Marian Anderson was born in Philadelphia in 1897. She adored her hardworking and devoted father. Her mother, a diminutive woman with a commanding presence and powerful strength of character, was probably the single most important figure in her life. Anderson began singing early in life with the junior choir of her church, and even as a child her deep rich voice, known musically as a contralto, did not go unnoticed. After being asked to sing for another local church, eight-year-old Anderson happened upon a poster for the concert with her picture on it, billing the child as a great attraction and stating excitedly, "Come and see the baby contralto!"

Church choirs continued to play a central role in Anderson's musical life through her teens and 20s. It was there that interested and admiring members of the church and community took it upon themselves to raise money to help Anderson pursue her musical dreams. She approached a musical school in Philadelphia and asked for an application. In one of the earliest instances of blatant racism she experienced from the music world, the teenage Anderson was icily informed that no black students were welcome or permitted to enroll. The shock of the rejection from fellow musicians stayed with Anderson for many years, but it did not affect her ambition.

When an exclusive teacher and singer named Guiseppe Boghetti agreed to take Anderson as a student, her church quickly raised the money to pay for the lessons. Under his tutelage, her confidence and abilities grew. She had been performing extensively for several years, and with Boghetti's help she began to book larger and more prestigious concerts. She traveled to Europe, and over the next few years she performed frequently and to great acclaim in Scandinavia, Germany, and Austria.

A high-powered and influential manager signed Anderson on her return to the states. She was booking increasingly larger concerts and touring constantly, though as before, she needed to know which hotels would welcome her and which wouldn't, which mode of transportation she would be allowed on and from which she was barred.

"When incidents occur in our land that show a disregard for brotherhood among races our America belittles herself, and her prestige is injured."

Anderson's growing reputation and the racial restrictions she encountered were bound sooner or later to create an explosion, and in 1939 they finally did. When Anderson's manager made inquiries about a concert in Washington's Constitution Hall, he was told in no uncertain terms that only white musicians could play there. This was decreed by the owners of the hall, the Daughters of the American Revolution (DAR)—a woman's patriotic society created by descendants of those who fought in the American Revolution.

One of the DAR's most highly visible members was Eleanor Roosevelt, the president's wife. Appalled by the DAR's racism, Roosevelt very publicly resigned from the organization in protest and was instrumental in arranging for Anderson to perform instead at the Lincoln Memorial. In what became a powerfully significant moment in civil rights history, some 75,000 supporters attended the concert.

Six years later, Marian Anderson was attending a party following the opening night of *Midsummer Night's Dream* at the Metropolitan opera in New York City. There, the general manager of the opera came over to say hello and casually asked Anderson if she would be interested in singing with the Metropolitan. Anderson's response, that she thought she would like to sing with them, was made to sound equally casual. But they both knew very well that this was a history-making moment. No black singer had ever been asked to sing as part of the Metropolitan company before.

The first performance of the opera *The Masked Ball* was highly charged with emotion, both from Anderson and the New York City audience, which included her mother. One week later, the Metropolitan Opera performed the same work in Philadelphia, and Anderson had the opportunity to make history again in her hometown, as the first black woman to sing with the Metropolitan Opera. Through her own sense of dignity and perseverance, and a voice the like of which is heard only once a century, she toppled barriers that would never completely rise again.

KATHRINE SWITZER

First woman to officially enter and run the Boston Marathon

1947–

Running the Boston Marathon has been a prime ambition for serious runners since its inception in 1897, when 15 runners entered the race. Today, registration is available for 20,000 runners. By the sixties, the Marathon was already a high profile event, but its contestants were limited to men only. In 1966, a woman named Roberta Gibb hid in the bushes near the starting line. She then joined the runners, and finished the race 126th out of about 500 entrants. But her run had to be made secretly and unofficially. The Amateur Athletic Union (AAU) prohibited women from competing in long distance races, subscribing to the curious belief that they were too weak and too easily injured.

As a child, Switzer was already drawn to athletics and displayed a natural gift for sports. She wanted to use her abilities to become a cheerleader, until her father challenged her on the subject, suggesting that it might be more fulfilling to participate in a sport rather than cheer in the background. His message made an impact on his 12-year-old daughter.

In 1967, 20-year-old Kathrine Switzer was attending Syracuse University and was a member of the men's cross country team. After her coach informed her that women could not run long-distance courses, Switzer went on a run with him. She did not stop until she had run 31 miles—her coach had stopped some miles back. Having proved to herself and her coach that the beliefs about women running long distances was false, Switzer traveled to Boston to tackle the Marathon.

Switzer completed her application for the 26-mile race giving her name as K.V. Switzer, and she dressed for the race in bulky, gender-disguising clothing. Having no hint that she was not a man, race officials registered her for the race and assigned her a number. At that time no one sold long distance racing clothes for women, so Switzer borrowed a pair of baggy running shorts from a man on the Syracuse track team, and she dyed them burgundy to match her shirt. She pinned her number, 261, to her shirt. When she began the race on the chilly April morning she wore a hooded sweatshirt, and easily blended in with the other runners. But when she pulled her sweatshirt off midrace, her secret was no more—she was a woman.

Enraged, a race official pursued Switzer. As he reached her, Switzer was horrified to find him attempting to rip the race number off of her shirt, as he shouted to her to get out of the race. As another racer urged Switzer to "run like hell," her boyfriend, ex-football player Tom Miller, shoved the race official away from Switzer. Shaken but un-hurt, Switzer continued to run. A photographer snapped shots of the ugly encounter. The pictures of Switzer and her boyfriend fending off the angry race official, which were published in newspapers across the country, speak volumes as to the ridiculous level that sexism in the Marathon had reached.

"I think my run was very important because of what happened. It showed the inequities that existed. And it changed my life."

The incident provoked such an outcry that the Amateur Athletic Union was forced to reexamine its position on women entering marathons. After a five-year battle, the AAU finally resolved the issue in 1971, revising their rules to permit women to run in all marathons sanctioned by their organization.

Since her famous unveiling in 1967, Kathrine Switzer has run 35 marathons countrywide, and in 1974 she won the New York City Marathon. In addition to running, Switzer went on to found the Avon Running Global Women's Circuit, offering running opportunities and events to women in over 21 countries. She also remains active in the movement to bring more women, especially women over 40, to the world of walking and running. She is the author of a book on the subject and remains firmly convinced of the endless benefits exercise offers to women, which include two of her favorites: "sanity and vanity."

FRANCES PERKINS

First woman to hold a cabinet position in the United States government

1880–1965

Born in Boston in 1880, Frances Perkins was raised in a financially comfortable family along with her only sibling, Ethel. Having inherited her father's intellectual curiosity and ability, Perkins attended Mount Holyoke College at a time when very few women had the means or ability to achieve a higher education. Her studies at Mount Holyoke required her to become familiar with the workings of local factories. The terrible working conditions, both unclean and unsafe, were shocking to Perkins. She saw firsthand that factory conditions themselves were a great contributor to poverty, particularly when they resulted in the injury of employees. It was at this time that her interest in the plight of the impoverished worker began to grow.

After graduating, Perkins wanted to work for a charitable organization but found she lacked the experience necessary to be hired. Instead, she taught school for the next five years, all the while remaining keenly interested in issues concerning industrial workers. In her spare time, she read all she could on the subject of the state of factories in local industry and its effect on the working class. In 1909, she went to New York City to undertake a research project investigating the conditions of poorly nourished schoolchildren. When she began to work for the New York Consumer's League she undertook similar projects, such as documenting the deplorable working conditions in local bakeries and factories. It was during this time that Perkins became instrumental in publicizing the 54 Hour

Bill—a proposed law that would restrict the factory work week to 54 hours or fewer.

Perkins experienced a staggering confirmation of her beliefs when she witnessed the fire at the Triangle Shirtwaist Factory in 1911. With only one elevator working and other exits blocked, 146 people died within the space of an hour, many of them leaping to their deaths from the eighth floor. Perkins, who had been nearby, saw victims jumping. The dead were mostly young immigrant women workers. A state commission was organized to conduct an official investigation. Perkins was hired as an investigator. The commission helped enact 36 new laws that set limits on work hours, provided worker protection, and rendered aid to employees injured at the factory.

When Al Smith was elected Governor of New York in 1919, he asked Perkins to work for the New York Department of Labor as a member of the Industrial Commission. Many openly voiced displeasure at the prospect of a woman being appointed to the position. Perkins was now married to economist Paul Wilson, and she was concerned that this might impact on the time she was able to spend with him and with their daughter, Susanna. Nonetheless, Perkins accepted the job and was sent to Oneida County to help settle a dispute between striking copper workers and their employers.

The workers were protesting their poor wages and the fact that they were made to work overtime without extra pay. They were frustrated and angry because no one in power would talk to them about making changes. Perkins not only

"I had more sense of obligation to do it for the sake of other women than I did for almost any other one thing. It might be that the door would close on them and that weaker women wouldn't have the chance."

talked to the striking workers but also listened to them. They trusted her, and Perkins was able to make a deal with them, buying the time needed to ultimately settle the dispute without violence.

When Franklin Delano Roosevelt was elected Governor of New York in 1928, he and Perkins began a long and gratifying working relationship. Roosevelt was very supportive of her work to pass laws that restricted child labor and imposed limitations on hours for women workers. When Roosevelt won the presidential election in 1932, he asked her to join his Cabinet, as the Secretary of Labor. Her feelings were mixed. She was happy working for New York State. Her husband was seriously depressed and recuperating at a New York sanitarium, and her 15-year-old daughter might not take to being relocated to Washington.

But many of Perkins's peers presented compelling reasons why she should accept the position. She could improve many lives by her work. And by accepting the position, she would become the first woman to obtain a position in the U.S. Cabinet, making history and creating opportunities for future generations of women.

She had never turned her back when she was needed. So in 1933, Frances Perkins became the United States Secretary of Labor. Programs such as the Works Progress Administration created jobs for needy millions. But perhaps the most famous was the Social Security Act of 1935. The idea that all workers were entitled to receive financial benefits while unemployed or after retirement was revolutionary. Today, our society depends on the notion that every worker is entitled to a measure of security.

Frances Perkins continued her crusade to defend the worker until President Roosevelt died in 1945. She was appointed to the Civil Service Commission by President Truman in 1946 and joined the faculty of Cornell University School of Industrial and Labor Relations. When she died in 1965 at the age of 85, Frances Perkins left behind a country permanently changed by the notion that a safe and clean working environment was the entitlement of every American.

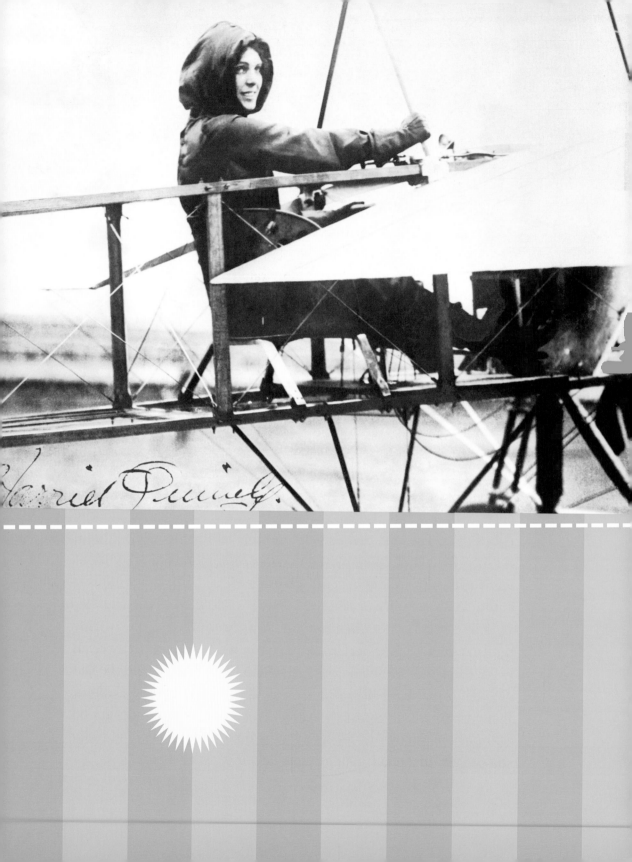

First American woman to obtain a license to fly

1875– 1912

In the history of aviation, it is Amelia Earhart who is most often remembered as the pioneering woman of the field. And yet two decades before Earhart's celebrated trans-Atlantic flight, the woman she called her role model, Harriet Quimby, was making headlines in her own right as America's first female pilot.

Harriet Quimby was born in Michigan in 1875, one of two daughters of farmers William and Ursula Quimby. Quimby was an intelligent and adventurous child with a reputation for being a tomboy. On completing her education, Quimby had no desire to marry and settle down. She decided to pursue a career in journalism. Quimby was resourceful and headstrong, and she found work in California and later New York as a reporter.

By 1903, Quimby began being regularly published by the magazine *Leslie's Illustrated Weekly*, writing on subjects ranging from human interest to theater reviews. She was a naturally gifted writer and had a knack for choosing engaging topics.

In 1910 her constant search for writing material brought her to the Belmont Park International Aviation Tournament in Long Island. Quimby later declared it was while watching the American pilot John Moisant win a race to the Statue of Liberty and back that she fell in love with flying. She began pursuing more articles about flying, and her interest in the subject soon became an all-consuming passion. She felt certain that she herself could learn to fly—if only she could find a pilot willing to give lessons to a woman.

It had only been eight years before, in 1903, that the Wright brothers had made their historic first flight. The subject of flying was a national favorite—it seemed that every month a new record was broken or a new stunt accomplished. Quimby convinced her editor at *Leslie's* that if the magazine arranged and paid for her to have professional flying lessons, the resulting articles she would write about the experience would be hugely popular.

Quimby's appearance at the Long Island flight school was newsworthy enough to be reported in the *New York Times*. She was right —the idea of a woman learning to become a pilot was of great interest to the public. Airshows showcasing the talents of the world's best pilots were enormously popular, frequently drawing tens of thousands of spectators. Aviation was still an unpredictable and dangerous business, and accidents and pilot deaths were not uncommon. The risk was part of flying, and it was accepted by pilots and spectators alike.

After nearly three months of study, Quimby was ready to take on the qualification tests. She passed, and became the first woman in America and the second in the world to receive a pilot's license. She was a celebrity, and now it was Quimby herself performing aviation feats before crowds. All the while she was nursing a new goal—to become the first woman to fly a plane across the English Channel.

"I felt like a bird cleaving the air with my outstretched wings."

Quimby traveled to France and purchased a plane designed by Louis Bleriot, a French pilot who was the first to fly across the Channel. On April 16, 1912, she landed on the coastline of France, having successfully repeated Bleriot's Channel crossing. It was a feat worthy of headlines, but there were none. The ocean liner *Titanic* had just sunk, and the attention of the world was focused on that disaster.

Quimby was fully aware of the enormous risks in flying, and the frequent accidents and deaths. She wrote on the subject several times in her magazine articles, stressing that safety procedures and the minimizing of risk-taking were crucial to making flying safe.

In July 1912, Quimby signed on to perform at the Third Annual Boston Aviation Meet. She was scheduled to make a flight to and from Boston Light, and at the last minute she agreed to take a passenger, event organizer William Willard. The flight around the light was uneventful, and Quimby circled back toward the airfield, flying over Boston's Dorchester Bay. In view of the landing field and thousands of spectators, the plane suddenly lost speed, the tail coming sharply up over the nose. As the horrified audience watched, Willard was pitched out of the open cockpit, and moments later, Quimby followed. The two fell, tumbling head over heels more than a thousand feet, into the shallow waters below. Just 11 months after becoming the first woman pilot in America, Harriet Quimby was dead.

The reason for the accident is a mystery. Some guess that there was a sudden mechanical failure to the aircraft. Others speculate that Willard, a large man, leaned forward to try to get Quimby's attention and unbalanced the delicate plane. Many presumed that neither Quimby nor Willard were wearing their seatbelts since they were thrown from their seats. Others, citing Quimby's constant insistence on safety before everything else, feel it is impossible she would have neglected to take this precaution.

The previous year, Quimby had written an article for *Leslie's* that eerily foreshadowed her own death. One paragraph began, "The fatalities of the air come so quickly and unexpectedly and the end is so sudden that the cause of the catastrophe is obviously left to surmise, so we have as many causes as there may be conjectures. None of them may be right. The aviator who falls a thousand feet or more rarely survives to tell of his misfortune."

PEARL S. BUCK

hen Pearl Sydenstricker was growing up as the daughter of a missionary in Asia, the landscape and culture of the Chinese people were as foreign to the average American as the surface of the moon. What to her were everyday scenes of peasants and farmers formed a lifestyle completely unknown to the West.

1892–1973

Though born in Virginia in 1892, Pearl Sydenstricker's future lay in the East, and the family returned to China when baby Pearl was only three months old. Her father, Absalom Sydenstricker, was a zealous and energetic evangelist, determined to dedicate his life to the conversion of the Chinese people to Christianity. He was a stern and rigid parent who held very traditional ideas of the role of women in society. His wife, Carie, was a dutiful if unhappy wife, and a devoted mother to her children.

Sydenstricker's recollections of her childhood in China include the constant knowledge that she was an outsider, both physically and culturally. She was taller than the average girl her age, with light hair and skin, and though her family had lived in China for years before her birth, they were still obviously Westerners when there were very few in the country. She had few friends, and became used to spending time alone, taking solace in reading books, both in English and Chinese.

It was largely a somber existence, both at home and outside. Four of the seven Sydenstricker children had died in childhood, leaving only Pearl and her younger sister, Grace, and her adult brother, Edgar.

It was not a joyful household. Outside, hostility abounded. The Chinese had deep-seated anti-Western feelings and were particularly unhappy with the missionaries such as Absalom Sydenstricker who believed that the Chinese were an inferior race who could only be helped by the teachings of Christianity. Pearl was also a young girl in an Asian culture that valued boy children above all else, and where baby girls were frequently put outside and left to die. The anti-Western feelings boiled over in 1900 during the Boxer Uprising, in which many missionaries and their families were murdered. The Sydenstrickers escaped with their lives and moved back to America for a year until the worst of the violence had passed.

Even as a child, Pearl Sydenstricker knew she wanted to be a writer, and the stories she had to tell to a Western audience were largely unique. When the time came for her to seek a college education, she went to America and attended Randolph-Macon Woman's College. But soon thereafter she returned to China and married an American missionary and proponent of agricultural reform, John Lossing Buck. It was then that she began to write, using as material the people and landscape of the impoverished and arid village in which they lived, Nanhsuchou.

As an adult now living in her own modest household, Buck began to see the Chinese people in a different way from the patronizing viewpoint held by her father. She found the treatment of women to be backward and often cruel, but she also discovered that the farming families were often intensely loyal, enduring, and honorable.

Though Buck was finding her writing voice, her home life was disintegrating. Her marriage was not a warm or supportive one. It was not a happy time, and when Lossing Buck received an invitation to teach in Nanking, he and his wife were both eager for the change. They moved to Nanking, but their family situation deteriorated further when their first child was born in 1921 with a condition that caused her to be mentally disabled. Because of complications during childbirth, Buck was unable to bear any more children.

Her life in China continued to be fraught with hardship, both at home and in Nanking. Buck created stories and articles from this chaos, and in 1930 her first novel was published. It was followed the next year by her second novel, titled *The Good Earth*. It was this book, based on what she saw living in Nanhsuchou, that captivated the Western world. *The Good Earth* immediately became a best seller, was adapted as a major motion picture, and won the highly coveted Pulitzer Prize. Buck would write constantly until her death in 1973, publishing over 70 books and becoming the first American woman to win the Nobel Prize for Literature, in 1938.

When she returned to America in 1934, she was active in many civil rights causes and continued in her endeavors to help the cultures of East and West come to know and understand one another. In 1941, she founded the East and West Association for this purpose, and in 1949 established an adoption service for Asian and mixed-race children called Welcome House. She ended her unhappy marriage to John Lossing Buck, and eventually married her publisher, Richard Walsh.

At the time of her death in 1973, Pearl Buck had almost single-handedly created a window between China and America, providing each with telling glimpses of the other, and fostering exchange and understanding between the two above all else.

> "The basic discovery about any people is the discovery of the relationship between its men and its women."

OLGA SAMAROFF STOKOWSKI

First American woman to debut at Carnegie Hall

1880–1948

Lucy Jane Olga Agnes Hickenlooper had arrived in New York City with her mother in the fall of 1904 with great ambitions but no connections. She was 24 years old and possessed of a magnificent ability as a pianist at a time when neither women nor Americans were given particular favor by classical music audiences. Hickenlooper was determined to launch herself into a career as a concert pianist, and what better place to begin than New York's renowned Carnegie Hall?

She and her mother rented a tiny room and with the forthrightness and sense of purpose that was a common trait of the women in their family, they set out to obtain an interview with Henry Wolfsohn, a highly influential and successful New York manager. To her dismay, Wolfsohn barely listened to her and would not even allow her to play. No pianist could debut in New York, he explained, without previous experience and reviews from Europe. Talent was inconsequential—without proof of European success, there was no hope.

As the dejected girl and her mother walked down the sidewalk mulling over what happened, Hickenlooper spotted Steinway Hall, where some of the world's greatest pianos were made and sold or rented. She dashed inside and was given permission to play. She sat at the keyboard and played furiously, displaying all her abilities and emotions on the instrument. In an incredible stroke of luck, at that moment Henry Wolfsohn himself walked into Steinway Hall and immediately demanded to know the identity of the pianist playing so brilliantly. For the second time that day, he came face-to-face with Lucy Hickenlooper. It was true she had never performed in Europe. But perhaps, Wolfsohn thought, an exception could be made.

At Wolfsohn's direction, Hickenlooper hired an orchestra and booked a date at Carnegie Hall. Paying for her own venue and musicians was the only way. It was a staggering amount of money to gamble, but she and her mother pressed on with the plan. Wolfsohn's last advice was for the pianist to change her name, and so Lucy Hickenlooper became Olga Samaroff. Though she was said to have taken the name from a distant relative, it is generally thought that she thought the name warm, easy to remember, and notable for its Russian sound. Samaroff chose an ambitious program of works to perform, and on January 18, 1905, the young woman gave her first New York concert. The following day Samaroff received a crucial endorsement—positive reviews from New York critics. She was on her way.

It was one of many high points in an extraordinary life. She was born in Texas into a financially comfortable family of absent men and strong, musical women. When she was 15, her grandmother took her to Europe to study the piano; she became the first American woman admitted to the Paris Conservatoire Nationale de Musique. She remained in Europe for almost five years, entering into an ill-fated marriage with a Russian who would later stalk her and threaten her through her years as a concert performer.

After her Carnegie Hall debut, Samaroff took engagements with other prestigious venues, such as the Boston Symphony Quartet in 1905. Her reviews continued to indicate she was a serious musician of extraordinary abilities. It was around this time that Samaroff met a young and unknown conductor named Leopold Stokowski. Their romance was slow to begin, but they eventually married, and with Samaroff's extensive musical and social influence, the young conductor eventually achieved a position conducting the Cincinnati

Orchestra. Though the marriage would not endure, Stokowski went on to achieve status as one of the world's most gifted conductors.

In 1920, under the baton of Leopold Stokowski, Samaroff became the first American pianist to perform all 32 Beethoven piano sonatas in concert. It was an important time for achievements by American musicians. Americans both as performers and audiences had previously been dismissed by most Europeans as unimportant. Samaroff helped to change that.

After her marriage dissolved, leaving her with a child to support, Samaroff turned to teaching to provide the money and stability she wished her daughter to have. She was offered a job at Julliard, a school that would soon attain the status of one of the country's best musical institutions. In taking the position she became the first American-born musician to become a member of the piano faculty. She taught at Julliard for 20 years and also established competitions and aid funds to assist American musicians.

She attained her own legendary status as a Julliard professor, and she continued to teach until the end of her life. She died at the age of 67, having influenced the lives of countless students who had come through her doors over the years.

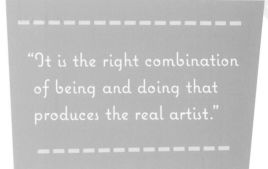

"It is the right combination of being and doing that produces the real artist."

In their memorial letter to the *New York Times*, some of those students described their teacher's spirit as "remarkably generous, vital and glowing." Each time they played, they continued to pay her tribute.

CARRIE CHAPMAN CATT

First woman to call for a League of Women Voters

1859–1947

She found her calling at the age of 13, when she asked her mother why she was not accompanying her father into town to vote in the presidential election. The answer young Carrie Lane received, that women were not permitted to vote, astonished her.

Born in 1859 on her family's Wisconsin farm, she was greatly influenced by her mother, an intellectual woman and early feminist. Determined at a young age to push herself, Lane taught school to earn the money she needed to attend college. She moved with her family to Iowa and attended Iowa State Agricultural College, working as a dishwasher for nine cents an hour to continue earning money to pay her tuition. At Iowa State she broke tradition and demanded the right to speak at the Crescent Literary Society, where spoken presentations were only permitted to men. Lane's demands to speak were eventually met, and she organized a debate on women and the vote. It was at this time that she began to develop her remarkable abilities as a public speaker. By the time she graduated in 1880, the subject of woman's suffrage, or right to vote, was central to her life.

Lane first intended to use her sharp intellect and public speaking abilities to become a lawyer, and again she took up teaching to earn tuition money for graduate school. But she found teaching so rewarding she gave up her plans to study for a law degree. It was while teaching in Iowa that she met her first husband, Leo Chapman, a journalist and earnest supporter of the woman's right to vote. By 1886, when the couple had married and decided to move to California,

Carrie Lane Chapman had already established herself publicly as an influential speaker, writer, and organizer for the cause of women's suffrage. But within days of arriving in California, Leo Chapman took sick with typhoid fever and died. Grieving and alone in a strange city, Carrie Chapman found work to support herself and focus her energy.

It was in California that she became reacquainted with George Catt, a classmate from Iowa State Agricultural College, and a fellow supporter of woman's suffrage. With his encouragement, she began to give speeches on social issues and was soon being asked to organize woman's suffrage clubs. Her popularity grew as she accepted more speaking engagements. In 1890, she acted as Iowa's delegate, or representative, at the National American Woman Suffrage Association (NAWSA) convention. At the convention she rubbed elbows with the luminaries of the suffrage movement, such as Susan B. Anthony, Elizabeth Cady Stanton, and Lucy Stone. The speech Carrie Chapman gave there, and the work she did for the movement in the following year, established her among the ranks of leading suffragettes.

Shortly after the conference she married George Catt, and the couple considered themselves a team working toward winning women the vote. Her reputation continued to grow, and in 1892 Susan B. Anthony asked Carrie Chapman Catt to give an address to Congress on the subject of a suffrage amendment to the Constitution.

> "How is it possible that a woman who is unfit to vote, should be the mother of, and bring up, a man who is?"

Catt was proving herself to be a highly competent organizer, and some of her most important work for the movement now involved bringing women together and laying out campaigns and speeches. It was slow and exhausting work, tackling the objective of gaining suffrage state by state. By 1896, only four states had given women the right to vote, Wyoming, Colorado, Utah, and Idaho. Following these gains, 14 years passed before another state passed woman's suffrage.

In 1900, Susan B. Anthony, now 80 years old, announced her retirement as president of the National American Woman Suffrage Association, and Carrie Chapman Catt was elected to the position. She remained president for four years, helping to create the International Woman Suffrage Alliance during her tenure. The years after her presidency ended were personally difficult. Catt lost both her husband and Susan B. Anthony, who died in 1905 and 1906, respectively. But she continued her work with the International Woman Suffrage Alliance, toiling year after year to spread the word and increase support.

In 1915, Catt resumed the position as president of NAWSA. The organization was finally drawing closer to its goal. Seven additional states had granted woman's suffrage, and by 1918, an additional four, including New York, were added to the rolls. At long last, in 1919, the 19th Amendment to the Constitution granting all women citizens of the United States the right to vote was approved by Congress. When the amendment was ratified in 1920, every woman in America of eligible age automatically had the right to participate in voting.

Though she had achieved the object of her life's work, Carrie Chapman Catt continued her work on behalf of women voters for the rest of her life, most notably founding the League of Women Voters. When she died in 1947 at the age of 88, the woman's crusade lost one of its greatest and most tireless activists.

1940–

The speedometer read almost 250 miles per hour when the inner tube flew out of her wheel and locked in the spokes, causing her racing dragster to career out of control. When she hit a culvert the car flew to pieces around her, and the impact was so powerful she was thrown hundreds of feet from the vehicle. She had fractured bones in her legs, pelvis, and hand, her foot had almost been ripped from her leg; and her thumb hung to her hand by a strip of skin. It was June 29, 1984, and the life of Shirley Muldowney, drag racing's top female performer, hung in the balance. After four months and six operations, doctors warned Muldowney to prepare for the possibility she might never walk again. They said racing would be out of the question. Those restrictions simply weren't acceptable to Muldowney. Eighteen months later, she was back behind the wheel on the racetrack.

Born in Burlington, Vermont, in 1940, Shirley Roque first learned to drive as a girl, sitting on her father's lap behind the wheel of the family Chevy. She fell in love with the sensation of driving, and by her mid-teens had commandeered her first drag racer—a 1951 customized Mercury that belonged to her boyfriend. Shirley and her boyfriend, Jack Muldowney, quickly developed legendary status as the fastest pair of racers in the area. When Muldowney turned 19, now married to Jack, she decided it was time for her to break into the world of professional racing.

Though she was not made welcome by other drivers or spectators, and was occasionally booed when she raced, Muldowney rapidly rose through the racing ranks. In 1965, she became the first woman to obtain a license to drive a gasoline-powered dragster from the National Hot Rod Association, and in 1973 that same group licensed her in the higher Top Fuel class, meaning she would now be driving the fastest race cars in the world. She mastered the complicated finer points of driving the rocket-shaped cars, which require lightning reflexes and reach such great speeds that it is necessary to deploy a rear parachute to slow them down.

Muldowney not only pressed on through the all-male ranks, she flaunted her gender, painting her race car hot pink and wearing a matching uniform and helmet. When Muldowney's car was on the track, it was clear to everyone in attendance that a woman was behind the wheel.

In 1977, Muldowney won her first National Hot Road Association championship in the Top Fuel class. She repeated her wins in 1980 and 1982 to become the first driver, male or female, ever to win the World Championship three times. The following year, 20th-Century Fox made a feature film about her life titled "Heart like a Wheel." It was shortly after the film was released that Muldowney suffered the devastating wreck that almost took her life.

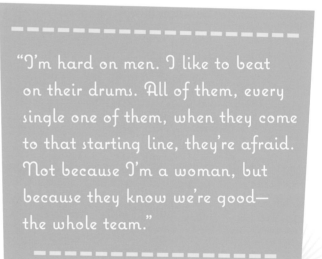

"I'm hard on men. I like to beat on their drums. All of them, every single one of them, when they come to that starting line, they're afraid. Not because I'm a woman, but because they know we're good— the whole team."

The accident had an effect on the racing world; wheels and tires were redesigned to specifically resist the kind of malfunction that had caused Muldowney's crash. And true to her word, Muldowney defied her doctors' predictions and both walked and raced again. In 1986, she completed her quarter-mile run in the fastest time of her career. By 1989, she had lowered her time even more, racing a quarter mile in 4.9 seconds, a rare feat for any driver and never previously accomplished by a woman.

Muldowney continued to race at top performance levels through the nineties and was honored by the New York State Senate when they included her in their display titled "Thirty Women of Distinction," alongside other accomplished women such as Eleanor Roose-velt and Susan B. Anthony.

Shirley Muldowney defied all expectations and broke down the barriers of dragster racing. She is the sport's top female star, and it is difficult to imagine anyone ever surpassing her accomplishments and tenacity.

First American woman to be ordained as a rabbi

1946–

In 1972, there were approximately one million members of the Reform branch of Judaism in the United States. One of them, a 25-year-old woman named Sally Priesand, was about to make history.

Sally Priesand was born in Cleveland, Ohio, in 1946. Intelligent and keenly interested in teaching, Priesand's parents taught her to set goals for herself that were both lofty and courageous. When her family moved to a different part of town, the teen-aged Priesand found that she and her brothers were the only Jews in their new high school. It was during this time that Priesand became more intensely involved with her temple and its youth group.

Priesand's parents encouraged her growing interest in her Jewish faith. They allowed their daughter to invite her non-Jewish friends to family observances such as the Passover seder so that she could teach them about Judaism. One year, Priesand's congregation awarded her a summer scholarship to the Union Camp Institute, run by the Union of American Hebrew Congregations. Priesand deeply felt the honor of having been singled out by her congregation. She later described the experience as a turning point in her life. It was the summer during which the idea of devoting her life to Judaism took root.

Priesand wanted more than anything else to be a teacher of her religion, and she knew there was no better way to do this than to become a rabbi. However, even within the relatively free-thinking Reform branch of Judaism, no woman had ever been ordained. When Priesand entered Hebrew Union College (HUC) in 1964, she was not the first female to do so with the intention of becoming a rabbi. But no one had yet succeeded. Many of her classmates assumed Priesand was only there to find a suitable husband. Because of her dedicated study, occasional speechmaking, and outspoken goal of becoming ordained, people began to take serious notice of her. Preisand became relatively well known while at HUC, often appearing as the subject of articles in newspapers across the country. However, there were still many who expected she would drop her lofty plans in favor of marriage as soon as the time came.

Priesand did not engage in arguments with those who opposed her goals. Instead, she preferred to focus on those who believed in her and what she was doing. One of her most crucial support-ers was Dr. Nelson Glueck, President of the Hebrew Union College. Some years earlier, he had stated that he was prepared to ordain any qualified woman who complet-ed the required course of study. In private, he told his wife that of the three things he wanted to do before he died, one of them was to ordain Sally Priesand. Sadly, his death came one year too soon.

> "In those days, I did not think very much about being a pioneer, nor was it my intention to champion the rights of women. I just wanted to be a rabbi."

On June 3, 1972, Sally Priesand was ordained by the new presi-dent of the college, Dr. Alfred Gottschalk. Her ordainment was national news, and a historic triumph for women. But for Priesand, there were more challenges ahead. Most importantly, she needed to find a congregation of her own. She got a job as an assistant rabbi but left when it became clear that she would never be promoted to the senior position. Her first 12 applications were rejected, nine of them without even an interview. At the time, she felt that a man with her qualifications and experience would not have experienced the same trouble finding a position. After several years Priesand did find a congregation of her own, first at Temple Beth El in New Jersey, and in 1981 at the Monmouth Reform Temple, where she has served as rabbi for some 25 years.

She was the first, but she did not remain the only American woman rabbi for long. Priesand had opened the door, and there were many qualified and ambitious women waiting to follow her through it. More than three decades after her historic ordination, women continue marching through.

JULIA MORGAN

First American woman admitted to the Ecoles des Beaux-Arts Architecture School

1872–1957

Julia Morgan came from a warm, well-educated family, financially secure because of her millionaire grandfather, though her own father failed in business ventures frequently. She was born in San Francisco in 1872, the second eldest of a family that would grow to include five children. Money was always available to the children, including the two girls, and no expense was spared on their education. Unlike most female students of the time, Julia attended school regularly in Oakland, California, all the way through high school.

She was a gifted student, intelligent, curious, and committed. At the time of her high school graduation, Morgan would naturally have been expected to enter Oakland's world of society by becoming a debutante. But Morgan had no intention of attending parties for the next year, and instead stated she would attend the University of California at Berkeley. With her parents' support, Morgan enrolled in many math and science classes at the university, often the only female in attendance.

By her second year she knew she wanted to use her gift for the sciences in a creative way—Julia Morgan decided to become an architect. With this goal in mind, she concentrated on engineering classes, and when she graduated in 1894, she was the university's only female graduate in the College of Engineering.

As someone who always aimed at the very highest goals, Morgan's next move was to seek entrance at one of the most prestigious architecture programs in the world—the Ecole des Beaux-Arts in Paris. No woman had ever been admitted to its architecture school, but Morgan was not discouraged. Ten years earlier Louise Blanchard Bethune had obtained membership in the American Institute of Architecture, making her the first American woman to practice architecture professionally. The barriers were falling, and Morgan intended to use the momentum to her own advantage.

She studied exhaustively for the exam, which was given in French, but failed to make a qualifying score on her first two attempts. On her third try, however, she succeeded, and entered the school. She completed the course of study in two years. At the age of 29, Julia Morgan became the first woman in the world to graduate from the architecture school of the Ecole des Beaux-Arts.

Triumphant, she returned to California and opened her own office. In the beginning, most of her work came from friends, including a wealthy young woman named Phoebe Hearst. One of Morgan's first major jobs was on the design team of John Galen Howard. Morgan's work was well received, and the team began designing a Grecian-style outdoor theater for the University of California. It was while working on this project that Morgan first met Phoebe Hearst's son, William Randolph Hearst. The work she would do for him in the fu-ture would gain her national recognition.

Passing the state examinations and becoming the first registered female architect in Califor-

> "My buildings will be my legacy. They will speak for me long after I'm gone."

nia, Morgan thought she was ready for anything. However, no one could have been prepared for the devastating earthquake that struck San Francisco in 1906. Over 20,000 buildings had collapsed, and a fire raged through the city for four days. The magnificent Fairmont

Hotel was still standing but had sustained serious structural damage in the fire. Morgan was hired to rebuild the grand building. Her performance and the quality of her work earned her the respect of her colleagues, and she had work wherever she wanted it from then on.

In 1919, Morgan received a visit from William Randolph Hearst that would result in one of the most celebrated constructions of her career. Hearst had amassed a fortune in publishing and had inherited an enormous amount of money and land on his mother's death. He wanted to build a house on some of his land in San Simeon, two hundred miles south of San Francisco. He wished to have a home designed to showcase his massive collection of art and furniture, much of which had been obtained from castles in England and Europe. For the next decade, the plan continued to unfold and come to life. By 1924, three guesthouses had been completed, and Morgan began work on the main house, called later by many "Hearst Castle."

It may well have been the greatest home in the country. With 144 rooms, the grand house contained a movie theater, a two-story assembly hall, and a refectory that could accomodate 30 diners. One of the grandest touches was the Neptune pool, a massive and elegant outdoor structure built to match the ancient Roman temple front that Hearst had purchased and had shipped to California.

Morgan continued to work on the San Simeon mansion and on projects for other clients until the 1940s. With the coming of World War II, supplies and manpower were in short supply, and Morgan was now in her 70s. Her health was failing. In 1951, around the time William Randolph Hearst died, Morgan closed up shop.

Julia Morgan died in 1957 at the age of 85, having reached the exclusive inner ranks of America's best architects. From modest apartment dwellings to the unbelievable splendor of Hearst's Castle at San Simeon, Julia Morgan achieved her dreams, and unlike many others who made castles in the air, Morgan built hers solidly on the earth.

GERTRUDE EDERLE

First woman to swim across the English Channel

The narrow sea separating France from Great Britain is a choppy sleeve of unpredictable currents and rough waters called the English Channel. The water can be bitterly cold and treacherous, and it is inhabited by jellyfish, Portugese man-of-wars, and every now and again a shark. As Mount Everest has tantalized mountain climbers for generations, so the English Channel has lured the world's best swimmers. At its narrowest point, the Channel is 21 miles across. In 1926, when Gertrude Ederle was 19 years old, many had tried to swim across it. Only five had succeeded. All of them were men.

Gertrude Ederle was born in 1906 to a German immigrant family. Ederle's fondness for the water was evident early in her childhood during seaside vacations, when she learned to dog-paddle while her mother held her afloat with a rope tied around her waist. By the time she was a teenager, Ederle had already proved herself to be an outstanding swimmer, and when she turned 17 she had earned a reputation as a breaker of world records and a winner of long-distance races. Her powerful performances earned her a spot on the 1924 U.S. Olympic swim team, and during the games in Paris, Ederle won a gold and two bronze medals. She returned home triumphant—and ambitious.

Ederle was one of the most visible and accomplished members of the Women's Swimming Association. That group funded Ederle's new dream—to be the first woman to swim across the English Channel. She made her initial attempt in the midsummer of 1925, but she was pulled from the water against her wishes by her trainer in the rescue boat when she choked on a mouthful of seawater. Ederle was angry at what had happened and determined to try again. Many swimmers made numerous attempts, some as many as thirty, before they successfully swam the Channel. Ederle was eager to try again, but the Women's Swimming Association could not afford to sponsor a second try. Fortunately she found a newspaper publisher willing to pay for her next attempt.

Early in the morning of August 6, 1926, Gertrude Ederle stood at the water's edge in Cape Griz Nez, France. She was wearing a black silk bathing suit made especially for her by her sister. She wore a red bathing cap and amber goggles, and her body was entirely covered with a greasy concoction of olive oil, lanolin, and lard. The coating, intended to defend her body against the frigid temperature of the water, would also serve as protection if she were to be stung by a jellyfish or a Portugese man-of-war.

Ederle plunged into the water and began to swim. The water was choppy but nothing Ederle felt she couldn't handle. However, after several hours, the weather conditions began to deteriorate. The wind picked up, and the waves grew in size. Conditions became rough enough that local steamship crossings were canceled. But

"I just knew if it could be done, it had to be done, and I did it."

there was no turning back now. Singing to the rhythm of her stroke to keep her spirits up, Ederle pressed on, even when the waves and current swept her back toward France.

A boat filled with her family, trainer, and some reporters followed Ederle, occasionally passing her chocolate and juice using a net on the end of a long pole. The food kept her energy up and the sight of her family strengthened her spirits, but there were times the current and waves were so powerful she was swept out of view of the support boat entirely. By late afternoon, the seas were so violent that several people on the support boat were incapacitated with seasickness. Fearing for her life, her trainer began calling for Ederle to give up. She shouted back her soon to be famous response—"What for?"

Shortly before ten o'clock that evening, 14 1/2 hours after setting out from France, Gertrude Ederle staggered out of the water and onto the beach at Kingsdown, England. Factoring in the additional distance she had swum against the current, Ederle had covered 35 miles to cross the 21 miles from France to England. And she had beaten the fastest man's time by almost two hours. The world was stunned by her accomplishment, and Gertrude Ederle returned to New York a national hero.

She was welcomed home with a massive ticker tape parade. Gertrude Ederle had become world famous, and she was quite literally the toast of the town. It was her finest moment. Ederle had suffered from hearing problems since early childhood, and her lengthy spell in the frigid Channel waters caused more serious damage, ultimately leaving her mostly deaf. In 1933, she fell down a stairwell and suffered a spinal injury that took years to heal. But Ederle never lost her resolve, learning to walk again, and giving swimming lessons to deaf children.

Her record-breaking swim made her a hero to Americans and women alike. But after her brief time in the spotlight, Ederle lived out her days quietly. Every so often a reporter would seek her out to write about her on the anniversary of her swim, but otherwise she seemed largely forgotten by the public. When asked, Ederle told reporters she had no complaints about her life and that she was comfortable and satisfied. She died at the age of 98 in a New Jersey nursing home. Still one of the greatest swimmers our country has known, her accomplishment remains a wonder of the sport to this day.

First writer of multivolumed metaphysical work
to be included in the Yale archives

1929–1984

One fall night in 1963, the writer Jane Roberts sat working on a poem when a startling transformation overtook her. She felt as if she had separated from her body, and her mind was suddenly confronted with a rush of information and ideas that were completely unfamiliar to her. When the sensation passed, Roberts opened her eyes and found that she had written down extensive notes on the ideas.

Roberts and her artist husband, Rob Butts, lived quietly in Elmira, New York, spending their days working, writing, and painting. They were hardly a couple likely to undertake an investigation of what seemed to be some kind of supernatural occurrence. Their beliefs were planted firmly in everyday reality. But the experience stuck with Roberts, and soon she and her husband were experimenting to see if any more information might appear. Since Roberts could not simply make the transformation happen again, they used a Oujia board—a board printed with an alphabet on which a clear disc was used to spell out possible messages from the supernatural.

The Ouija board worked, and soon Roberts found the information coming into her mind before the words appeared on the board. So they set the board aside, and in a state of extreme focus and detachment from her surroundings, called a light trance state, Jane began dictating the material to Rob, who wrote each word down in shorthand. In trance, Jane identified her speaking personality as Seth. Seth eventually began to dictate his material as books. Little did Roberts realize that evening's session would be repeated twice weekly for the next two decades.

Jane Roberts was born on May 8, 1929, in Saratoga Springs, New York. She lived with her mother, who was an invalid due to severe rheumatoid arthritis. Her mother's condition became so severe that Roberts was sent to live in an orphanage for two years. When she returned home, the care of her mother fell largely on her shoulders. Jane turned to writing poetry to express her feelings.

In 1954 Roberts married the artist Robert Butts. They settled in Elmira and worked various jobs to provide enough income to allow them to pursue their creative work at home. By the time Jane began speaking for Seth in 1963, she had published several science fiction novels and many poems. She would continue to write fiction and poetry along with working on the Seth material, though her own work took on a similar metaphysical theme.

The definition of *metaphysical* is something relating to a reality that is beyond what we normally perceive with our physical senses. Prayer, ESP, and hauntings are all metaphysical topics. Though some Eastern cultures have incorporated metaphysical ideas into their religion and philosophy for centuries, these ideas were relatively new to western civilization and were generally considered by most of the public to be outlandish. Unlike today, when bookstores devote entire sections to what we now lump together as New Age works, in the 1960s the subject was not one that was likely to bring financial success. But Jane Roberts would not, or could not, abandon the subject.

The premise of the Seth material was simple enough—we create our physical reality, from the smallest rock to the most significant life event, through our thoughts and feelings. What we concentrate on, we get. If we believe the world is full of dangerous situations and violent people, and look for this reality at every turn, than this is the world we encounter. Another person living in the very same world who believes the world is a safe and loving place filled with mostly kindhearted people will encounter that reality at every turn. In other words, each human creates his or her reality, one completely unique to what that person believes and expects. Today, there are many schools of metaphysical thought that include this basic premise.

The Seth material provided many scientific and religious ideas that Jane Roberts had no knowledge of. Was Seth in fact a "personality essence" as he described himself, a person who existed as a kind of ghost outside our physical reality system? Or was the information coming from some hidden area of Jane Roberts's consciousness? Roberts herself never fully accepted either explanation. The material spoke for itself—its value was obvious regardless of the source. Roberts only wanted the question of Seth's origin to be examined—by her, by her readers, by her skeptics. For she felt the act of examination itself, the probing and questioning the limits of our consciousness, was the entire point of Seth's teachings.

"The imagination, backed by great expectations, can bring about almost any reality within the range of probabilities."

Jane Roberts died in 1984 of complications from rheumatoid arthritis. Twenty years after her death, more than 30 books, both by Seth and by Roberts herself, are in print. Over seven million copies of them have been sold around the world. The original shorthand notes taken more than two decades by Robert Butts are housed in the Yale archives, and each year more of the previously unpublished material is being put into print. For each student of metaphysics or each skeptic who studies the papers and wonders at their origin, another door into the mystery of our reality is opened.

GEORGIA O'KEEFFE

First woman given a retrospective exhibition by New York's Museum of Modern Art

1887– 1986

orn on a Wisconsin prairie farm in 1887, Georgia O'Keeffe's earliest memories are of being taken outdoors as a baby and seeing the brilliant hues of greens and blues glowing with sunlight. Her passion for the natural world and her abiding love of landscapes would last a lifetime and fuel one of the most brilliant art careers in American history.

She knew as a child that she wanted to be an artist, and at the age of 12 she took her first painting lessons. Her talent was immediately obvious, but in spite of her declaration, it was almost unheard of for a young girl of this period to pursue a career as an artist. When she was 13, O'Keeffe was enrolled in Wisconsin's Sacred Heart Academy, a boarding school that emphasized drawing equally with other studies. The following year her family moved to Virginia and O'Keeffe was withdrawn from the school. But the foundation of serious artistic instruction was secure in the young painter.

During the next six years O'Keeffe was able to study painting both at the Art Institute of Chicago and New York's Art Students League. But events kept bringing her home to Virginia. When she contracted the often deadly typhoid fever in the summer of 1906, she was bedridden for months. She spent the year at home recovering her strength. When she was better, O'Keeffe pursued teaching positions to support herself, taking classes when she was able.

In 1916, while teaching in South Carolina, O'Keeffe sent a number of charcoal drawings to her close friend in New York, Anita Pollitzer. Without O'Keeffe's knowledge, Pollitzer promptly brought the drawings to the renowned photographer Alfred Stieglitz. A prominent gallery owner and champion of artists experimenting with new creative forms collectively called avant-garde, Stieglitz was well known to O'Keeffe as one of the most influential figures in modern art. When a student in New York, she had visited his gallery many times.

Stieglitz was extremely impressed with what he saw, and he displayed the pictures in his gallery, bringing the unknown O'Keeffe immediately into the limelight. He convinced her to move to New York, and so began one of the most important personal and artistic relationships in the history of modern art. Stieglitz was widely acknowledged to be a giant in the artistic field,

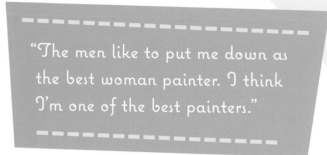

"The men like to put me down as the best woman painter. I think I'm one of the best painters."

and his support and growing passion for O'Keeffe, evidenced by the hundreds of photographs he took of her, led her to increasing fame.

In 1918, O'Keeffe moved to New York to pursue her career as a painter. Stieglitz, 24 years her senior, left his wife. He and O'Keeffe were deeply entwined both romantically and artistically, and in 1924 they were married. By this time, O'Keeffe's reputation as an extraordinary artist was already established, though she bristled at being defined as the country's most successful "female" painter.

Her interpretations of the world, from skyscrapers to enormous brilliantly colored flowers, crossed barriers in style and approach as she constantly experimented with new ideas and subjects. Her summers with Stieglitz in New York's Lake George produced some of her most important landscapes, but it was upon visiting New Mexico for the first time that O'Keeffe felt herself come truly alive as a painter. The altitude, the quality of the light and the massive empty countryside inspired her in a way she had never felt before. She frequently visited the state, and eventually purchased property there. After Stieglitz died in 1946, she moved to New Mexico permanently.

She was not a social person, and though she had close friends she cherished her solitude in the vast state and the underpopulated town of Abiquiu. Throughout her life her appearance was unconventional and striking. She was small and lean, with powerful bony features and long hair pulled back in a tight knot. She favored simple, black dresses and preferred to live with almost no decorations or ornaments in her home. As she moved through her 70s and 80s, O'Keeffe seemed to become a physical symbol of the culture around her— weathered and undecorated, timeless in her beauty.

O'Keeffe's delight in the landscape of New Mexico and the vistas of her own imagination are everywhere in her paintings. From her famous depictions of bleached animal skulls adorned with flowers to her thoughtful, almost obsessive paintings of the patio door and wall near her studio, her sense of joy and peace in her surroundings is evident.

In 1970, the 83-year-old painter was given a retrospective exhibition by the Whitney Museum of American Art. She had already become the first woman, some 24 years earlier, to be given her own restrospective exhibition at New York's Museum of Modern Art. The 1970 exhibition continued at the Art Institute of Chicago and later the San Francisco Museum of Art. Record-breaking crowds viewed the paintings, and O'Keeffe reached heights of fame she had never known before. Over the next 15 years she was awarded the nation's Medal of Freedom, a Radcliff College lifetime achievement award, and the National Medal of Arts.

But as always, what O'Keeffe most wanted was to be alone in her New Mexico home and to paint. She was able to do exactly that until shortly before her death at the age of 98, in 1986. O'Keeffe best described her success and happiness herself—she knew what she wanted to do and did it.

KATHLEEN MCGRATH

First woman to command a U.S. Navy warship

1952–2000

Just a decade earlier, it would have been unthinkable. Only a few years had passed since Congress lifted the ban prohibiting women from serving on warships or any combat aircraft. Now, in 1998, five Navy women had been selected to command ships. Four of those women were assigned to transport vessels, ships not expected to enter a combat zone. But the fifth woman, Kathleen McGrath, received command of the U.S.S. warship *Jarrett*. It was an appointment heard around the world. Captain McGrath had shattered a barrier of massive proportions.

She was born near Columbus, Ohio, at an air force base, daughter of Air Force veteran James McGrath, who had flown B-52 combat missions over Vietnam. Her childhood was spent mostly on Air Force bases in Texas, New Mexico, and as far away as Guam—where she graduated from high school. McGrath's ambition at this stage did not include the armed forces. She graduated from college with a degree in environmental science and began working with the U.S. Forest Service. After several years she began to question the opportunities the Forest Service could offer her, and her father suggested she look into the Air Force.

She did, and in a fluke of Armed Forces history, the Air Force recruiter happened to be out to lunch when McGrath stopped by at his office. There was a staffed Navy office nearby, so McGrath went in there instead. The travel and adventure the recruiting officer described to McGrath sounded appealing. So she joined the Navy rather than the Air Force, and the rest, as is so often said, is history.

Though the Navy still held very strong beliefs about the limitations of women in the service, they were gradually beginning to place women in positions of more authority. McGrath attended naval officers school and received her commission, or military rank. After being admitted to the Surface Warfare Officer's School, which took very few women, McGrath was able to gain a wide scope of experience serving on different ships. Her success working on ships called support vessels resulted in her being given command of a rescue and salvage ship in 1993. It was around this time that she began to dream of commanding a warship.

In 1998, her dream came true when she was given command of the warship U.S.S. *Jarrett*. One of the smaller ships in the navy, the *Jarrett* is equipped with massive firepower, including anti-aircraft weapons, both air and water missiles, torpedoes, and a special pair of Seahawk helicopters that can perform a variety of combat or rescue functions.

In the year 2000, McGrath and her crew of 262 patrolled the northern waters of the Persian Gulf to hunt for smugglers moving oil from Iraq against the express order of the United Nations. She also led the search and rescue operation for Alaska Airlines flight 261, which had crashed in nearby waters with 88 people aboard. There were no survivors.

Commanding a warship is a lonely and demanding job, and McGrath's days often began before 6 a.m. and continued past midnight. In addition to the enormous responsibility she bore to her crew, McGrath also had a family at home that she missed terribly. Her husband, Greg Brandon, a retired Navy officer, remained at home full time to take care of the couple's two adopted children, who were ages 2 and 3 during the *Jarrett's* six-month assignment. Both Brandon and McGrath believed they were doing the right thing to give McGrath this opportunity. Their son thought that everybody's mother worked on board a navy ship.

When Kathleen McGrath completed her six-month mission commanding the *U.S.S. Jarrett*, she began serving at the Joint Advanced Warfighting Unit in Alexandria, Virginia. Only 48 years old, she had already won four Meritorious Service Medals, three Navy Commendation Medals, the Legion of Merit, and a Navy Achievement Medal. If her life had not been cut short by cancer two years later, there is no telling what she might have gone on to achieve, though it is hard to imagine her improving upon her already extraordinary performance in the military, as a commander and as a trailblazer for women.

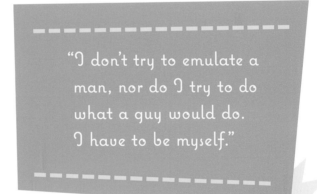

"I don't try to emulate a man, nor do I try to do what a guy would do. I have to be myself."

FANNY BULLOCK WORKMAN

First woman to summit Pinnacle Peak in Kashmir

1859–1925

It is unknown if Fanny Bullock Workman's childhood dreams included scaling snow-covered peaks halfway across the world. She was born in 1859 into a well-to-do and socially prominent Massachussetts family. When Bullock was seven, her father was elected Governor of the state. Though her family's security gave Fanny Bullock great freedom in life, she was still a female child of the Victorian age. Girls of this period had strict limitations set on their activities, and the richer the girl the greater the number of guidelines set by society. Dresses were heavy and difficult to wear—corsets were laced as tight as possible around a woman's middle, giving the illusion of a tiny waist and preventing much comfortable movement. The customs of the time controlled girls and women through clothes, in homes that were expected to be the center of their worlds, and in a culture that expected them to be quiet and obedient. But Fanny Bullock was not to be kept in one place all her life.

When she was 22, Fanny Bullock married a successful and well-respected doctor named William Hunter Workman. She may have looked poised to take on the role of wife, hostess, and member of polite society. But when Dr. Workman retired from his medical practice seven years later, the couple decided to travel abroad. Their young daughter remained at home with a nurse. The Workmans spent the next several decades touring through exotic locations and writing books about their experiences. They began in Europe, using the newfangled bicycle as their mode of transport. Though the bikes were heavy, and Fanny Workman rode wearing the long full skirts of the time, the couple sometimes biked 70 miles in a single day. After traveling through Spain and Algeria, they took a boat to India, crossing the subcontinent on their bikes over the course of the next several years.

It was during this time, in Kashmir, that Fanny Bullock Workman had her first glimpse of the world's most awe-inspiring mountain ranges—the Himalayas and the Karakoram. As so often happened, both husband and wife were of the same mind—why not give up bicycling and begin climbing these fortresses? In Europe, Workman had gained her first serious experience as a climber, ascending mountains such as the Matterhorn, still considered a challenge to mountaineers today. She felt ready to tackle the ranges of the world's largest mountains.

During their initial trips around the area hiking or riding ponies, the Workmans brought large numbers of porters along to carry their food and gear. They had difficulties getting their wishes across, as they spoke no Hindustani and did not understand the ways and customs of the locals. But they were undaunted—their fascination with the massive mountains inspired them to lead six trips into the ranges over the next 14 years. Many areas were unmapped and had never been visited by a Western woman. Workman helped to fill in the blanks on the maps, sending geographical information that she recorded to England's Royal Geographic Society.

"When, later, woman occupies her acknowledged position as an individual worker in all fields, as well as those of exploration, no such emphasis of her work will be needed; but that day has not fully arrived, and at present it behooves women, for the benefit of their sex, to put what they do, at least, on record."

In 1899, Workman and her husband summitted Mount Koser Gunge, and standing on its peak at 21,000 feet, Fanny Workman broke all known altitude records previously held by women. She had become powerfully strong, and her body was growing accustomed to climbing in the thin air of the high altitudes. The couple organized at least one expedition a year, not only exploring and mapping remote areas and glaciers but also putting together scientific data and taking photographs. When Workman climbed and reached the top of the Nun Kun Massif's Pinnacle Peak, she broke her own climbing record and set a dazzling new one that a later survey measured as 22,810 feet. A trailblazer in almost every area except that of dress, Workman made the climb in full skirts.

Fanny Bullock Workman held the social and political beliefs one might expect for a woman so unrestrained by society. She believed deeply in women's right to the vote and in women's equality, and she was a proud tradition breaker. Her travel books often detailed the customs and experiences of women of other cultures. She was also fiercely competitive, and when the American Annie Peck announced she had reached an altitude of 23,000 feet climbing a mountain in Peru in 1908, Workman had researchers sent to Peru to measure the mountain. When the group's findings estimated the mountain to be approximately 1,000 feet lower then Peck's guess, Workman had the findings published in *Scientific American*. Workman's place as the woman who climbed the highest was, for the moment, secure. But through her own example she opened the door for the many women mountaineers who would follow in her footsteps, and ultimately climb even higher.

EVE QUELER

First American woman to conduct at a major European opera house

1936–

At the head of every orchestra is a conductor, bringing together the efforts of each musician and instrument to perfectly perform a musical score. Of all the positions in the world of musical performing arts, that of conductor is one of the most difficult for a woman to obtain. One of a handful of American women who has successfully gained entry to this exclusive club is Eve Queler.

Born in New York City in 1936, Queler was a musically inclined child who began studying the piano at the age of five. While attending New York's High School of Music and Art, Queler added the French horn to her studies, and she continued to immerse herself in music at the Mannes College of Music. It was there that the appeal of choral music and the human singing voice took root in Queler. She indulged this growing love by playing the piano to accompany singers.

After completing her training at Mannes, Queler knew that what she most wanted was to conduct. But this was much more easily dreamed than done. It was the 1960s, and the world of conducting was overwhelmingly dominated by men. It was impossible to pursue a professional conducting career without substantial experience, and as a woman Queler found that experience almost impossible to get. She had found a job as a pianist accompanying singers in New York's City Opera, but any conducting she was able to do had to be limited to rehearsals only. At the time, women were not permitted to conduct performances.

Effectively barred from conducting opportunities in New York's major orchestras, Queler decided to create her own experience. She organized an amateur symphony, purchased some music, and began to rehearse operas in concert (rather than fully staged) form. What began as a small and simple venture gradually grew in size and reputation. Her Opera Orchestra became known for performing operas that were little known or rarely performed. They developed a loyal and growing audience,

> "The burden of proof is upon us as women. We can't tell people we're good. We have to show it every time we conduct."

often selling out performances at New York's famous Carnegie Hall. More than 30 years after founding the Opera Orchestra, known in New York's musical circles as OONY, Queler has conducted more than 75 operas. She was the first American woman to guest conduct at a major European opera house, appearing in Nice, Barcelona, Australia, and the Frankfurt Opera, to name a few. In her own country, she was the first American woman to conduct the Philadelphia, Cleveland, and Montreal Symphony orchestras.

Over the years, she has been instrumental in discovering many new singers, and has worked with top world performers such as Jose Carreras, Rene Fleming, and Plácido Domingo. She has achieved a wide measure of critical acclaim, but even now there are those in the still conservative field of music who do not approve of women conducting.

Queler's accomplishments are not limited to bringing little-known works and singers to New York audiences. Through the inroads she and fellow women conductors such as Marin Alsop have made, women are slowly gaining ground in the field of conducting. It may be a long time yet before the sight of a woman on a podium wielding the conducting baton is common. And there are a limited number of major conducting positions available, making for very fierce competition. But the career of Eve Queler proves it can be done, and that is enough to inspire women to pursue this elusive dream.

RITA DOVE

1952–

Rita Dove's childhood in Akron, Ohio, was filled with books. Her father was a chemist, and her mother was a homemaker, both the first in their own families to earn educational degrees. The couple owned shelves upon shelves of books, which were always available to Dove and her siblings. From novels to poetry, from fairy tales to classics, Dove devoured them all, loving the feel and smell of the books almost as much as the words within. Some of her fondest childhood memories are of spending hours browsing through her parents' volumes or visiting the public library and savoring the freedom to borrow any book she desired.

She made the natural progression from reading to writing, and as a child she composed many stories and poems. Though she loved the act of writing, Dove later recalled that she never considered it something she might do as an adult. She equated writing with play, something a person did for enjoyment in her spare time. To Dove, writers were just faded names on the spines of books. She continued to feel this way until her 12th-grade teacher took her to a book signing to meet the poet John Ciardi. It was this experience that caused Dove to realize that writers were actual people, that they lived regular lives, and that there was no reason she herself should not become a writer, if she chose. That same year, Dove was chosen along with a hundred other students nationwide to be a Presidential Scholar. Young, highly intelligent, and ambitious, she saw unlimited possibilities in her future.

By the time she was a junior in college, Dove knew she wanted to become a poet. Her parents, who were not poetry readers themselves, nonetheless supported her ambition. Powerfully influenced by the importance her parents placed on learning and education, Dove applied herself to her studies with intense energy. She graduated from the University of Miami with the highest achievable academic honors and then studied at a German university as part of the Fulbright Scholar Program. When she returned to the United States after two semesters, she was fluent in German and ready to immerse herself in the University of Iowa's graduate program in writing.

In Iowa Dove met the man she would later marry, a German-born writer named Fred Viebhan. After graduating, Dove accompanied Viebhan to Oberlin College in Ohio where he had just gotten a teaching job. There she finished a collection of poetry that would be published in 1980 under the title *The Yellow House on the Corner*. Not tied down to a single location to write, Dove and

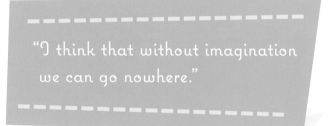

"I think that without imagination we can go nowhere."

Viebhan moved again after he left Oberlin. They lived in Jerusalem for a short time, when Viebhan was invited there to a writer's colony, and later in Germany. But after a time Dove realized she was developing a language problem that affected her writing. Her knowledge of German was overtaking English to the point where she even thought in German, and speaking and reading in her native language became increasingly difficult. The couple decided to return to the United States, and Dove obtained a teaching position at Arizona State University.

It was in Arizona that Dove completed *Thomas and Beulah*, a collection of poems about the lives of her maternal grandparents. In 1987, the book was awarded the Pulitzer Prize for Poetry, and Dove was thrust into a hectic new schedule of speeches and interviews and book tours. When her life finally began to slow back down, Dove and her husband and young daughter moved again, to North Carolina, into a beautiful house that looked out onto the Blue Ridge Mountains. There, in addition to teaching, Dove wrote and practiced her viola de gamba, a large stringed instrument similar to the cello.

Dove established a new rhythm in her life, productive and successful in her work and her play. But her life changed again in 1993, when Rita Dove was appointed Poet Laureate and Consultant in Poetry of the Library of Congress. Dove was the youngest poet ever to receive such an appointment, and the first African American. The Poet Laureate is appointed on a yearly basis by the Librarian of Congress to celebrate and promote poetry in the United States. Though it would mean another storm of requests, speaking engagements, and traveling, Dove eagerly accepted the opportunity to represent one of her greatest loves—the written word.

Dove served as Poet Laureate for two years, and the list of awards and honors she has received is enormous, including the Carl Sandburg Award, the Year 2000 National Book Critics Circle Award, and the 2001 Duke Ellington Lifetime Achievement Award in the Literary Arts. She has received over 20 honorary degrees from universities. Her profound creativity is not limited to poetry: Dove has also published fiction, had a "verse drama" produced and performed across the country, and written the lyrics to accompany a number of musical compositions, including a collaboration with composer John Williams and Steven Spielberg for a White House Millenium production in 1999.

Somehow between all of her writing projects, speaking engagements, and educational work, Dove also finds time to practice her viola, train her classical singing voice, and indulge in ballroom dancing. Her creativity truly knows no bounds.

HELEN KELLER

1880–1968

The woman whose disabilities would later make her world famous was born a healthy hearing and sighted baby in Alabama in 1880. The eldest child born to Captain Arthur Henley and Kate Keller, Helen spent the first year of her childhood in a home surrounded by gardens. She was a curious and intelligent child who was said to have a vocabulary of several words before her first birthday. One of those words was *water*.

When Helen became gravely ill with a high fever, the family doctor feared the worst. However, Helen began to recover after several days, and her parents were thrilled that in spite of their fears, Helen was not going to die. But though Helen became strong again, she seemed different. Her mother soon realized the source of the change. The illness they called a "brain fever" had left Helen completely blind and deaf. Only 19 months old, young Helen Keller was in an unreachable prison.

In the 19th century, gravely handicapped children such as Helen were usually institutionalized, sent away for life to a hospital or asylum. It is likely that Kate Keller was expected and even advised to send Helen away to such a place. She would not or could not do it. Helen remained at home, living a wild and unmannered existence, while her parents sought help. There was no medical solution for Helen. But one doctor gave them some very valuable advice. He knew of another child who was blind and deaf like Helen. Her name was Laura Bridgman, and she had been taught to read and to write.

If one such child could be educated, perhaps Helen could as well. The doctor advised the Kellers to seek the advice of an expert on the education of the deaf—an inventor named Alexander Graham Bell.

Bell was famous for his invention of the telephone, but his life's work had become educating the deaf through the teaching of lip-reading and speaking methods using a series of symbols called Visible Speech. He directed the family to the Perkins Institution in Boston, where Laura Bridgman had been educated. There, a young partially blind woman had recently graduated her course of studies and was ready to seek employment. Her name was Annie Sullivan, and with the school's recommendation, the Kellers hired her immediately.

Helen Keller later described March 3, 1887, as the most important day she remembered in all her life. It was the day Annie Sullivan arrived to teach her. Their first meeting did not go well. Six-year-old Helen was defiant and violent. But the teacher was no shrinking violet. With her physical strength, determination, and patience, Miss Sullivan was more than a match for Helen. Her first major victory was teaching her reluctant student to display proper table manners at meals. But even this victory paled in comparison to Miss Sullivan's next accomplishment. Through exhaustive repetition and daily reinforcement, Helen one day came to understand that the word *water* being spelled into her hand was a symbol for the real water running from the pump. As Helen herself later described it, it was the moment her "soul was set free." With the door to communication unlocked, Helen learned at an astonishing rate.

> "So I try to make the light in others' eyes my sun, the music in others' ears my symphony, the smile on others' lips my happiness."

By the age of eight Helen could understand more than 900 words, could write using a special stencil writing board, and could absorb all the works of literature Miss Sullivan spelled into her hand.

Clearly, she had an enormous intellect, and always she was eager to learn more. One of her greatest desires was to attend college. Together Helen and Miss Sullivan attended classes to prepare for the rigorous college examination.

Even for a healthy sighted and hearing girl, a college degree was not expected or even encouraged. The education of women focused more on the domestic realm, and a woman pursuing higher education was considered eccentric at best. For a blind and deaf girl, it seemed an outrageous proposition. But Helen and Miss Sullivan both possessed a steely determination. Since most textbooks were not available in the raised Braille print for the blind, Miss Sullivan spelled the books to Helen. In addition, Miss Sullivan attended all of Helen's classes, sitting alongside her student and translating the lessons into sign language in Helen's hand. The work paid off, and Helen passed her entrance examinations. Four years later Helen graduated from Radcliffe College—the first deaf and blind person ever to do so.

This was only the beginning for Helen. There was a great deal that she wanted to accomplish. While still at Radcliffe, she had written a memoir, and she would continue to write articles and books for much of her life. She toured the country with Miss Sullivan, making appearances and presentations in an effort to educate others about blindness and deafness. By this time, she was famous throughout the country and much of the world.

Though Helen Keller was utterly devastated by the death of Annie Sullivan in 1936, she nonetheless remained committed to speaking, writing, and educating on the subjects of deafness and blindness. And she was a key member of the American Foundation for the Blind, raising funds and constantly searching out new methods of helping others, particularly those who, like her, were deaf-blind.

Helen died in 1968, at the age of 87. The urn containing her ashes was laid to rest next to Annie Sullivan.

ANTONIA NOVELLO

1944–

As a child, Antonia Coello was no stranger to the world of medicine. Born in the Puerto Rican town of Fajardo in 1944, she suffered from congenital megacolon, a painful and abnormal condition of the colon that could not be corrected without surgery. Fajardo was not a wealthy town. Coello's divorced mother was a schoolteacher and later the principal of a nearby high school. Because she had neither time nor money to spare, she was unable to travel to a hospital that was large enough to offer the kind of surgery her daughter needed. Instead, Coello endured frequent stays in the local hospital to relieve the symptoms of her disorder. Unfortunately, this was always only a temporary measure, and before long she would become sick again. There was no system in place to help Coello, and she was not able to receive corrective surgery until she was 18 years old. She later said she felt this delay in her surgery was simply because she had "fallen through the cracks."

After her operation, Coello attended college at the University of Puerto Rico, in spite of the fact that she had to wear diapers for six months following the colon operation. Her extended experience as a patient, and her firsthand knowledge of the shortcomings of local medicine in Fajardo, instilled in her a desire to become a doctor. She was determined to prevent other children from falling through the cracks of medicine.

Coello applied to the University of Puerto Rico Medical School, but fearful of rejection, she did not tell her schoolteacher mother of her plans until she received the university's official acceptance. She received her medical degree in 1970 and married Navy Flight Surgeon Joe Novello. Ready to begin her residency training, Novello found her own childhood experiences of illness still very fresh. She felt a particular kinship with sick children. Accordingly, when she began her residency at the University of Michigan, it was in pediatrics, specializing in diseases of the kidney. Her work there was so successful she was named Intern of the Year, the first woman at the university to receive this distinction.

After completing her residency, Dr. Antonia Novello opened a pediatric practice in Washington, D.C. Because she was so committed to children's health, she found the daily work with gravely ill children to be emotionally traumatic. Several years later, she gave up her practice and began work with the Public Health Service, a government organization. Here Novello could devote her vast energy and intellect to developing programs designed to prevent sickness. She found she had a great talent working to combine the fields of law and medicine. Writing laws was one very effective way to help change Americans' unhealthy habits that would later cause disease.

> "I want to be able to look back someday and say 'I did make a difference.' Whether it was to open the minds of people to think that a woman can do a good job, or whether it's the fact that so many kids out there think that they could be me, then all the headaches and the chicken dinners will have been worth it."

The extent of Novello's abilities and intellect received ultimate recognition in 1989, when President George Bush nominated her to become Surgeon General of the United States. Novello eagerly accepted the position. The Surgeon General, sometimes described as the symbolic doctor to every American, wields the greatest influence on health and medical policies and laws. Because Novello had a personal interest in children and pediatrics, she focused a large part of her work on young people. Her office was decorated with dolls, photos, and drawings children made for her. Because of complications from her health problems, Novello had no children of her own. When she had the time, she visited children in local hospitals, making time for chats or hugs. Her official work also revolved around children. She was especially concerned with children afflicted with the AIDS virus. She also worked tirelessly to improve health care for those who were not receiving all that they needed, specifically minorities, women, and children.

Novello's work as Surgeon General was often controversial. Not everyone agreed with her programs. Her campaign against alcohol advertising appealing to young people had many opponents. She also launched an attack on the selling of cigarettes to consumers who were underage. She practiced what she preached by eating a healthy diet, taking frequent walks in the little spare time available, and chiding her brother-in-law, *Saturday Night Live* writer/performer Don Novello, for smoking on television as part of his character Father Guido Sarducci.

Antonia Novello's tenure as Surgeon General ended in 1993, and since then she has continued to work and write about the health issues about which she is most passionate. But her influence during her time as Surgeon General was not limited to the programs she began. As the first woman and first Hispanic to be Surgeon General, Antonia Novello was a daily reminder to women, Puerto Ricans, and anyone facing a life limited physically or financially of exactly what can be accomplished in this country.

BRENDA BERKMAN

1951–

Before 1977, there were no women in the Fire Department of the City of New York (FDNY), for the simple reason that women were not permitted to apply. When testing was opened to women that year, none of the applicants could pass the physical strength exam, which had been designed to test the strength of men. Was the test an appropriate and fair evaluation of potential firefighting skills? Brenda Berkman did not think so, and she brought a lawsuit against the department, resulting in a 1982 ruling that the test was discriminatory and did not work to fairly identify who was qualified for the job of firefighter. The ruling was a victory for women who sought to become firefighters, but it was only the first step in a battle that would continue for years.

Brenda Berkman was born in Asheville, North Carolina, in 1951, and moved with her family to Minnesota when she was only three months old. Her life was comfortably middle class, with her mother staying at home while her father, a veteran of World War II, worked at the post office. Berkman was a good student and hoped to be the first in her family to attend college. Her dream was realized when she was admitted to St. Olaf College, and though she describes the institution as placing an emphasis on service, young women were nonetheless not encouraged to go into firefighting.

While Berkman was in college, the tennis player Billie Jean King took a man named Bobby Riggs up on his challenge to prove that he could beat any female tennis player. In the resulting 1973 match, Billie Jean King emerged the victor, proving Riggs wrong. The

match, and its significance in improving the treatment of professional women athletes, was extremely influential on Berkman. Berkman
had experienced discrimination in sports early on at the age of nine,
when she was excluded from the local Little League because she
was a girl. From that time on, Berkman always resented the exclu-
sion of people with ability from opportunities simply because of
artificial constraints and biases.

After graduating from St. Olaf summa cum laude, meaning with
the highest academic distinction, Berkman went on to the New York
University School of Law. In New York she married a fellow lawyer
and worked at his father's law firm, one that represented the
firefighter's union. Through that work, Berkman began to meet firefighters, and she was impressed by how much they loved their jobs.
She realized that many
aspects of the firefight-
ing job fit what she
wanted to accomplish in
her life, including a
desire to help others and
to have a job where she
would be physically active.

> "How many fires do I have to go to before people take me and other women seriously as firefighters?"

While still a law student, Berkman took the FDNY entrance
exam. Berkman, along with every other woman that applied, failed
the physical endurance test. Berkman persuaded a prestigious law
firm to take on her suit against the fire department. The suit was
decided in Berkman's favor, and the fire department was required to
redesign the physical exam. As Berkman was to learn, the lawsuit
turned out to be one of the easier steps to becoming a firefighter.

In 1982, having passed the modified FDNY test, Brenda Berkman
was one of 40 women appointed as probationary firefighters. But her
fight was far from over. During her probation period, Berkman
endured extensive harassment from male firefighters who resented
her presence in the service. Following her evaluation by the company

captain, Berkman and another female firefighter were ordered dismissed from service. Berkman was devastated, but certain that her dismissal was the result of discrimination, she turned again to the courts.

In December 1983, a federal judge found extraordinary evidence of harassment and discrimination against both women and ordered them reinstated to the department. The written ruling went on to level serious criticism at the way in which the fire department had handled the addition of women on the job. At last, Berkman was allowed to perform the job for which she had proven she was qualified. Though the harassment she experienced from male firefighters diminished over time, it has never completely disappeared.

Berkman is now a captain and has been with the fire service for over 20 years. She was the founding president of the United Women Firefighter's organization and has led the national organization of women firefighters, Women in the Fire Service. In 1996, Berkman became the first professional firefighter to serve as a White House Fellow in the Office of the Secretary of Labor.

On September 11, 2001, Berkman had the day off, but the moment she heard that a plane had hit the World Trade Center, she rushed to her firehouse to gear up and help. She worked around the clock digging through the rubble and working with fellow rescue crews to search for survivors. Of the more than 400 rescue workers who lost their lives at the scene, 343 were members of the FDNY.

In spite of the obstacles and dangerous situations she has faced, particularly what she went through on the job on September 11, Berkman would encourage girls to pursue careers as firefighters if they feel qualified. At a time when there are only about half the number of women in the FDNY as there were in 1982, it is clear that the battle to remove discrimination in firefighting is not over. But thanks to women like Brenda Berkman, the tide has turned.

LAURA INGALLS WILDER

First writer to win the American Library Association's Laura Ingalls Wilder Award for substantial contribution to children's literature

1867– 1957

On February 7, 1867, a baby girl was born in a cabin deep in the woods of eastern Wisconsin. The cabin was the first of many places her family would call home. Over the next several decades, the places and events the girl experienced would form the basis for some of the most beloved and bestselling children's books of all time. The girl's name was Laura Ingalls, and the nine books she wrote about her life would become known as the Little House series.

The original little house was a modest log cabin in the forests of Wisconsin's Pepin County, built by Ingalls's father, Charles Ingalls, known as Pa, and her uncle Henry Quiner. The woods teemed with game for hunting, and Lake Pepin was full of fish. In addition to trapping and hunting, Pa provided for his family by farming and trading furs. The family had everything they needed, but like so many pioneers of the time, Pa felt the call of the west and wanted to move. Ingalls would come to share her father's restless nature.

The Homestead Act of 1862 provided would-be pioneers with the opportunity to claim and settle 160 acres of land, provided they lived on it for at least half of each year for a period of five years. If they met those and other requirements, they could eventually take ownership of the land they had claimed, free of charge. Pa found the opportunity irresistible. In 1868 he sold his property and the Ingalls family traveled southwest by covered wagon over 500 miles. They lived first on a farm in Missouri, then continued west to a claim just south of Independence, Kansas. The family settled on the vast, treeless prairie and lived there for two years before learning that their claim lay within Indian territory rightfully belonging to Osage Indians. Disappointed but undaunted, Pa took his family back to Wisconsin's Big Woods in 1871 and was able to buy back his original cabin and land. When Ingalls wrote about these two years, she shifted the timeline and consolidated the Pepin years into one stay. The stories of living in the Wisconsin woods and the Kansas prairie are contained in the books *Little House in the Big Woods* and *Little House on the Prarie*.

In Pepin, Ingalls's cousins and grandparents were nearby, and family life was comfortable. But with the coming of more people, it was harder to hunt for the game they relied on for food and fur. Pa was growing restless and was eager to take his family to a less populated area. In 1874, the Ingalls moved on again. This time they traveled directly west. Ingalls loved their Plum Creek farm near the Minnesota town of Walnut Grove. But the Ingalls family lost their crops to swarms of ravenous grasshoppers. They could not make a living on the farm, and soon they were on the move again.

After spending some time in Burr Oak, Iowa, and briefly returning to Walnut Grove, the Ingalls family moved one last time, to stake a claim in the Dakota Territory town of DeSmet. The constant moving had not always been easy on Ma and Ingalls's sisters, Grace, Carrie, and Mary, the eldest girl who went blind from what was probably scarlet fever. DeSmet seemed to have a future, and it was here that Ingalls's family finally settled down for good, allowing Laura Ingalls to meet her future husband, farmer Almanzo Wilder.

"I wanted the children now to understand more about the beginning of things, to know what is behind the things they see ... what it is that made America as they know it."

Laura Ingalls and Almanzo were married in 1885 and lived in DeSmet for the next four years. But bad luck coupled with Wilder's own restless nature caused the couple and their young daughter, Rose, to move on, first to Minnesota, and ultimately to Mansfield, Missouri. After years of hard work, Laura and Almanzo Wilder's Rocky Ridge Farm in Mansfield grew to 200 acres. Their daughter Rose was exceptionally intelligent, and after finishing school she traveled and found work, first as a telegraph operator and later as a journalist. At home, when she was not involved with housework and farming duties, Wilder wrote too, and she began to publish articles in the local Missouri paper. By 1915, the now married Rose Wilder Lane was sending letters to Laura encouraging her writing.

In her early 60s, Wilder began to work on an autobiographical book about her childhood. With Rose's help, Wilder later revised the book for a children's audience, using her memories of the log cabin in Wisconsin and the life her family had lived there. Harper and Brothers bought the manuscript, and the book was published under the title *Little House in the Big Woods*. The book did well enough for the publisher to ask Wilder to write a second book, and the Little House series was born.

By the time Wilder finished writing *These Happy Golden Years*, she was 76 years old and ready to retire. The Little House books continued to grow in popularity year after year. She received scores of letters each year from devoted readers, swelling to over a thousand on her birthday. In 1954, the American Library Association honored Wilder by creating in her name an award for writers who had significantly contributed to the field of children's literature. The first recipient of the award was Laura Ingalls Wilder herself.

Wilder died in 1957, at the age of 90. Her last book, *The First Four Years*, was published after her death. In the decades that followed, the interest and appetite for the Little House books continued to grow, as new generations of children eagerly jumped at the chance to glimpse America's pioneer past.

DIAN FOSSEY

First woman zoologist to study mountain gorillas
in their habitat

1932–
1985

From the time she was a child living in San Francisco, Dian Fossey dreamed of traveling to Africa. In 1963, when Fossey had been working for nine years as an occupational therapist in Louisville, Kentucky, she finally realized this dream, taking out a loan to finance the trip. She read constantly on the subject of Africa as she prepared to go. One book that found its way into her hands was George Schaller's *Year of the Gorilla*, the only study ever made of the elusive mountain gorillas of central Africa. Fossey determined to find these gorillas.

On the way, she stopped at the Olduvai Gorge camp in Africa's Serengeti National Park and met the legendary anthropologist Dr. Louis Leakey. His fossil discoveries had been instrumental in pinpointing the origins of the human species. Leakey took a liking to Fossey and was intrigued by her ambition to visit African mountain gorillas. Leakey's interest would eventually change the course of Fossey's life. Before returning to America, Fossey traveled to the Congo and had her first glimpse of mountain gorillas. She was so transfixed by her brush with the gorillas she would never be the same. Though she had to return home, Fossey was now consumed with the dream of returning to Africa to study the elusive mountain gorillas.

When Dr. Leakey gave a lecture in Louisville in 1966, Fossey attended. Not only did he remember her, he made her an extraordinary proposal. Leakey had been searching for someone to undertake a long-term study of the central African mountain gorilla. Leakey wanted someone without previous field training, since he felt such a person would have a completely open mind to his methods. His instinct told him Fossey would be perfect for the job. Stunned with her good fortune, Fossey accepted the position, and prepared to move to Africa.

The volcanoes that form the mountain chain of the Virungas reach into three African countries: Uganda, the Congo (later called Zaire, and today called the Democratic Republic of the Congo), and Rwanda. Fossey first made camp in the Congo area of the chain. But the Congo was in a period of unrest. A rebel group took control of the area, and soldiers forced Fossey to leave. She had to start her work all over again in another area of the Virungas, this one falling within the borders of the country of Rwanda.

Fossey established her Karisoke Research Center in a high meadow between Mount Karisimbi and Mount Visoke in September 1967. From the outset, Fossey realized that local poachers, people indulging in illegal hunting, were going to be a problem. Though the area fell within the protected Parcs des Volcans, poachers nonetheless set traps for antelope and hyrax, often snaring gorillas by mistake.

Through extraordinary patience, physical endurance, and her understanding of how to make her presence unthreatening, Fossey was gradually able to draw closer to gorilla groups. In the first days of 1970, accompanied by photographer Bob Campbell, Fossey lay in the foliage surrounded by the gorillas she designated as Group 8, making soothing sounds and gestures to reassure the animals. As Campbell filmed, one of the gorillas approached Fossey and extended his fingers to touch Fossey's hand. It was the first recorded instance of a mountain gorilla and a human being in a friendly physical encounter.

But Fossey was also making enemies. Stopping poachers became as important to her as studing the gorillas. In addition to hunting, poachers were often hired to obtain baby gorillas for zoos. They tracked groups, killing all the adult gorillas before snatching the infant. When Fossey's favorite gorilla, the intelligent and gentle

Digit, was found slaughtered in 1978, Fossey declared outright war on the poachers. She destroyed traps, confiscated weapons, burned the poachers' belongings, and offered money for their capture. For the gorilla victims of poachers, including Digit, Fossey created a cemetery near her camp. To finance her continued fight against the poachers, she established the Digit Fund in the gorilla's memory.

In 1985, Dian Fossey was found murdered in her cabin. No suspect was ever convicted. An American member of the Karisoke staff was suspected by Rwandan authorities, but many people believe the real killer was an angry poacher. Fossey was buried next to her beloved Digit. The future of her work, her gorillas, and everything she had fought for and given her life for was bleak.

Today the picture is more encouraging. The Digit Fund, now called the Dian Fossey Gorilla Fund International (DFGFI), still exists. A 2004 press release from the DFGFI reported that a recent census of Virunga gorillas showed a 17 percent increase in population since 1989.

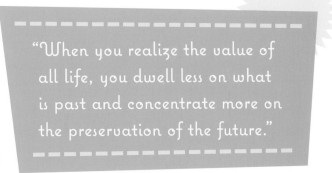

Dian Fossey feared that Digit had died in vain. The final entry in her journal reads in block letters: "When you realize the value of all life, you dwell less on what is past and concentrate more on the preservation of the future." The continuation of her work two decades after her death and the increased numbers of mountain gorillas in the Virungas are cautious grounds for optimism that Fossey's dream of saving the mountain gorillas can still come true.

SACAGAWEA

First Native American woman accorded the right to vote in an official U.S. government venture

c. 1790–?

On November 1805, a bedraggled group of explorers on the Pacific Northwest's Columbia River decided their next move by casting votes. Among the voters were a black slave and an Indian woman. The woman's name was Sacagawea. Sacagawea's vote was requested and counted by the Corps of Discovery, an official U.S. expedition organized by President Jefferson himself.

Sacagawea was born around the year 1790 in the Lemhi Shoshone tribe of the Rocky Mountains. As a girl of 11 or 12, Sacagawea was captured by the Hidatsa. She was kept captive until she was given her freedom several years later and adopted by the tribe. She remained with the Hidatsa, near the upper Missouri River in present-day North Dakota and became the wife of the French Canadian trapper Toussaint Charbonneau. Sacagawea was still living there when Lewis and Clark arrived in the area with their Corps of Discovery in December 1804 and built their winter quarters.

The Corps of Discovery, the brainchild of Thomas Jefferson, was the major geographical, scientific, and cultural exploration of its time. Charged with exploring the wilderness from the Missouri River west to the edge of the continent, the Corps would travel more than two thousand miles, much through unexplored territory. When they left their winter quarters in the spring of 1805, Lewis and Clark intended to look for the Shoshone tribe, which they had heard might be able to trade horses for the expedition's treacherous crossing of the Rocky Mountains. But they did not speak the Shoshone's language and were not sure where to find them. When Lewis and Clark met the trader and learned his Shoshone wife came from the very territory they were heading for, the Corps immediately hired the couple as guides and interpreters.

Virtually all facts that we have about Sacagawea come from the journals kept by Lewis and Clark. We know that before leaving the Hidatsa village, Sacagawea went into a difficult labor during the birth of her first child. Lewis administered her a potion, and shortly afterward the child was safely born. It is likely this episode created a bond of mutual respect between Sacagawea and her new employers.

The Corps departed the winter camp with Sacagawea, Charbonneau, and their new baby son, in early April 1805. They passed the conjunction of the Yellowstone and Missouri Rivers, battled river rapids in present-day Montana, and came to an astonished halt at the Missouri river's Great Falls, an 80-foot cascade of seething water.

Sacagawea was not the heroine that legend has made her out to be, particularly as she has been portrayed in 20th-century works of fiction wherein she literally guided the expedition all the way to the Pacific. However, it is true that she was essential to the well-being of the Corps. She contributed through her knowledge of edible plants and berries, her connection to the Shoshone people, and the peaceful intentions her presence with the Corps indicated to other Indians. In encountering tribe after tribe as the Corps pushed west, Indians gave the strangers the benefit of the doubt because an Indian woman was willingly accompanying them. But it was in passing into the territory of the Shoshone that Sacagawea became indispensable.

> "The wife of Shabono our interpetr we find reconsiles all the Indians, as to our friendly intentions a woman with a party of men is a token of peace."

It was crucial that Lewis and Clark obtain Shoshone horses to help their men cross the Rocky Mountains before colder weather arrived. But the Shoshone were elusive and wary of strangers. Lewis could make no headway communicating with them or obtaining their trust until he brought Sacagawea to see them. What followed was more than anyone had hoped for. Not only were the Shoshone the Corps had encountered Sacagawea's kinsmen, their chief was her brother. Now that a bond of blood and language was established, relations grew warm and the Corps got their horses.

As the winter of 1805–06 approached, the Corps strove to reach the Pacific Ocean and build winter quarters. When they reached their goal in November, they were jubilant. They had crossed the continent, mapping land no U.S. citizen had ever before seen.

Lewis and Clark now only had to decide where to make winter camp. They put the matter to a vote with each Corps member having equal say. Sacagewea was given the same voting privileges and power as each man in the Corps. In acknowledging Sacagawea's equal value and contribution to the expedition, Lewis and Clark and their Corps of Discovery made history by including her as an equal voter.

When spring came, the Corps began retracing their steps across the continent. After their return to St. Louis, Missouri, in September 1806, Sacagawea's story again becomes hazy, lost in time. We know that Clark eventually became foster father to the baby born to Sacagawea and Charbonneau at Fort Mandan. Sacagawea herself was said to have died in her mid-twenties at a trading post in today's South Dakota. But another story circulated that Sacagawea had lived on to the age of 100, dying in Wyoming in 1884.

Most of the facts of Sacagawea's life and death are forever lost. And yet her story continues to inspire us through books, stories, films, and songs. Though no one knows exactly what Sacagawea looked like, her image is reproduced in paintings, statues, and a U.S. coin. The indelible impression she made on the men of the Corps of Discovery lives on through the centuries.

EDNA ST. VINCENT MILLAY

First woman awarded the Pulitzer Prize for Poetry

1892–1950

By the time she had composed the poem "First Fig" in 1918, with its tantalizing image of a woman as a candle burning fast and fierce, Edna St. Vincent Millay was already an acclaimed poet and a notoriously romantic rebel.

Born 26 years earlier in Rockland, Maine, Millay and her two younger sisters were raised by their mother, Cora Buzzell Millay. Cora raised her three daughters single-handedly in nearby Camden. In spite of a shortage of money, Cora made certain her girls always had plenty to read.

As a young teenager, Millay began writing her own poems and submitted them to *St. Nicholas'* magazine for competitions. Cora, ambitious and unconventional, encouraged Millay in her writing, convinced that her daughter possessed a rare poetic genius. In 1912, Cora learned of a poetry contest being sponsored by the publisher Mitchell Kennerly. The poem Millay submitted, "Renascence," deeply impressed the judges of the contest and won fourth prize.

In the fall of 1913, Millay began her freshman year at Vassar College at the age of 21. Four years later she received her degree and moved to New York City. Her first poetry collection, *Renascence and Other Poems*, was published by Mitchell Kennerley in 1917. The volume was received with great critical acclaim, and Millay had begun an artistic ascent that would not taper off for well over a decade.

By all accounts, Millay simply captivated many who met her. Barely over five feet tall, with thick curly red hair and green eyes, the milky-skinned Millay seemed more fairy than human. Men and women alike fell deeply in love with her, and sometimes she with them. She was fully aware of her magical effect on others, and she delighted in it.

In 1923, Millay learned her latest poetry collection, *The Ballad of the Harp-Weaver,* had been awarded the Pulitzer Prize, making her the first woman to receive one of the nation's most prestigious awards for writing. The title poem was about and dedicated to her mother, Cora Millay.

Both Millay's personal and artistic lives seemed complete when she married the Dutch businessman Eugen Boissevain. Ill with stomach problems, Millay was admitted to the hospital for surgery immediately following her small wedding. It was the beginning of a cycle of bad health that would plague her, on and off, until she died.

Millay and Boissevain purchased a farm in Austerlitz, New York, which they named Steepletop. One of the first works she completed at Steepletop was the libretto, or song text, for Deems Taylor's opera *The King's Henchman*, which opened at New York's Metropolitan Opera House in 1927. That same year, Millay learned of the fate awaiting the Italian born Nicola Sacco and Bartolomeo Vanzetti. Sacco and Vanzetti were anarchists, members of a group with radical, antigovernment beliefs. When they were convicted of a robbery and murder in 1921, the case gained national attention. Many sympathizers feared the two had been unfairly prosecuted because of their anarchist political views. When Sacco and Vanzetti were found guilty and sentenced to death, Millay joined demonstrations on their behalf. In spite of the passionate pleas and public uncertainty regarding their guilt,

My candle burns at both ends;
It will not last the night;
But ah, my foes, and oh, my
friends—It gives a lovely light!
"First Fig"

Sacco and Vanzetti were executed in August 1927. Millay wrote about the episode in her poem "Justice Denied in Massachusetts."

Millay continued to receive high praise for the work she published throughout the next decade, during which time she was elected to both the National Institute of Arts and Letters and the American Academy of Arts and Letters. Though deeply shaken by her mother's death in 1931, Millay traveled with Boissevain to New York to promote her new book, amid a flurry of publicity. The country was in the middle of a devastating Depression, and money was scarce, but Millay's books sold at record levels. Within months of its publication in 1931, the collection *Fatal Interview* had sold over 50,000 copies, remarkable for a book of poetry even by today's standards. Her readings were often standing room only, with crowds of several thousand gathering to hear her famous voice. In 1943 she received the Gold Medal from the Poetry Society of America.

In 1944, Millay, constantly in pain from injuries sustained in a car accident, had become addicted to the painkiller morphine. She suffered a nervous breakdown and wrote practically nothing until 1946, when she resumed work on her poetry. But she had not regained her fiery zest for life. She primarily rested at Steepletop, cared for by her beloved and devoted husband. In 1949, Boissevain died shortly after an operation for lung cancer, and for perhaps the first time in her life, Millay was truly alone. She died just over a year later at Steepletop, after apparently falling down a dark staircase in the middle of the night, breaking her neck. During her life she blazed with brilliance. Like the candle burning at both ends she wrote of in 1918, Millay's life was extinguished too soon. However, her work and reputation continue to prosper, and Edna St. Vincent Millay is today considered one of the great American poets.

MARTHA GRAHAM

In a career that spanned more than seven decades, Martha Graham is considered to be not only the mother of modern dance but also one of the greatest artists and original thinkers of the American 20th century.

1894–1991

Born in 1894 in Allegheny, Pennsylvania, Graham was the oldest of three girls. When Graham was a teenager, her family moved to California. Her life was forever changed in 1911, when her father took her to Los Angeles to see a performance by the celebrated dancer Ruth St. Denis. From that moment on, Graham's heart was passionately given over to dance, and would remain so to the end of her long life.

Ruth St. Denis had abandoned the rigorous discipline and structured form of ballet. Inspired by legends of Indian, Greek, and Egyptian deities and goddesses, she choreographed and performed her own dances and was famous for her exotic interpretations of Eastern goddesses and customs. Along with her husband, the dancer Ted Shawn, St. Denis founded the now legendary dance school named Denishawn. In 1916, having graduated from the Cumnock School of Expression, Martha Graham enrolled in Denishawn at the age of 22.

She was not initially a standout, and St. Denis's first impression was that Graham was "totally hopeless." Ted Shawn later admitted St. Denis felt Graham was too heavy, too plain, and too old to be a successful dancer. Dogged and patient, Graham worked until Shawn told her she could outdance every other student in his class. Martha's calling as a soloist was now evident.

After several years, Graham herself was teaching classes at Denishawn, and she also acted as manager when the school company went on tour. Seven years after enrolling, Graham left Denishawn and took a job in New York City in the Greenwich Village Follies. Her performances made her one of the most successful dancers on Broadway, but after two years, she left the Follies, determined to strike out on her own. She was 30 years old, and she would continue dancing for another 40 years.

She worked teaching the Denishawn technique, but Graham was not content for long in teaching the dance methods of others. Encouraged by Denishawn's former musical director, Louis Horst, who had also struck out on his own, Graham abandoned established dance techniques altogether. She debuted her own dance group in 1926, producing 29 original dance works that year alone.

In 1929, Graham premiered a work now considered one of her first masterpieces, entitled "Heretic." The dance was a stark portrayal of a free-spirited individual, danced by Graham wearing white, who is oppressed by the rigid and anti-individual masses, danced by the chorus in black. Now teaching her own classes from a studio on New York's Tenth Street, Graham inspired passionate devotion from her students, who labored ceaselessly to mirror Graham's expression of all emotions as originating in the spine and torso.

Graham herself was the personification of the expressive physical form. Lithe and muscular at just under five feet three inches, she had an angular face and long, glossy black hair that beautifully accentuated her every movement. Behind her elegant appearance, Graham carried a famously explosive temper that cowed others, leading her on at least one occasion to hit one of her dancers.

To dance as Graham choreographed required massive physical strength. Unlike ballet, where the ground is used as a springboard, Graham's technique embraced the floor, using frequent spirals and slow falls. In her 1935 dance "Frontier," Graham used for the first time a simple but flexible set designed by Isamu Noguchi. The set added a third dimension to the stage, allowing an entirely new direction of movement for dancers.

Graham's work gained her a prestigious Guggenheim Fellowship in 1931, an award of cash enabling her to more easily pursue her art. She was invited to perform for President and Mrs. Roosevelt at the White House in 1937. Along with Louis Horst, she taught at Bennington College in Vermont. But her primary passion was in performance. Decade after decade saw Graham and her company remain ascendant on the dance stage. Though Graham featured company members in solos, including Eric Hawkins whom she would later marry, her own role remained that of the supreme soloist. For Graham her technique and choreography was completely intertwined with her own performances.

In spite of the misgivings of friends and colleagues, and the less forgiving admonishments of professional critics, Graham continued to perform until 1968, when she danced in public for the last time in the aptly titled "A Time of Snow." Finally, she conceded to the ravages of old age and retired from performance at the age of 75.

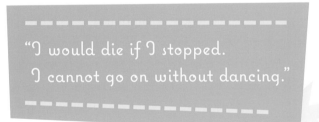

"I would die if I stopped. I cannot go on without dancing."

After suffering a physical and emotional collapse in the wake of her retirement, she rallied to return to work as the director of her dance company. She continued to teach and choreograph.

Martha Graham died in 1991 at the age of 96. Since first seeing Ruth St. Dennis dance 80 years earlier, Martha Graham remained consistently committed to the world of dance—a world now virtually inseparable from her name.

KATHARINE GRAHAM

First woman to head a Fortune 500 company

1917–2001

When Katharine Meyer was born in 1917, the business of journalism was an exclusive boys' club almost entirely off-limits to women. Meyer was the fourth of five children born to Eugene Meyer, a wealthy broker and financial genius, and his wife, Agnes. The family lived in luxurious surroundings even by today's standards, occupying mansions in Washington, D.C., and New York. In 1933, Eugene Meyer changed the direction of his life and career by buying the newspaper the *Washington Post*.

During her freshman year at college, Meyer began reading the *Washington Post* every day and writing letters to her father discussing the paper. In spite of her interest, Meyer had no misconception that the *Post* held any future for her personally. As the only boy in the family, it was her brother Eugene III, called Bill, who was expected to one day take over the running of the newspaper. However, Meyer became increasingly convinced that his son Bill was neither interested in nor suited to running the *Post*. He encouraged his daughter to pursue her interest in journalism. Meyer took a job at the *Washington Post* working on the editorial page.

In the fall of 1939, Meyer met a brilliant and mesmerizing young law student named Philip Graham, and they were married on June 5, 1940. Eugene Meyer asked Philip Graham to consider coming on board at the *Post*, with a view toward eventually taking it over. Both husband and wife were pleased at the prospect. Katharine Graham had thrived working as a journalist, but now that she was married she wished to focus on remaining at home to have children and run a household. Her husband immersed himself in the life of the *Washington Post*, becoming a highly respected newspaperman, and a friend and sometime adviser to President John Kennedy. Graham's home looked all but perfect to the outside world, but Philip Graham began to suffer from manic depression, characterized by alternating periods of frenetic activity and euphoria and paralyzing episodes of depression. In 1963, Philip Graham entered a psychiatric hospital. On leave from the hospital that August, he committed suicide as his wife napped in another room.

Following the shock of her husband's suicide, Graham was faced with deciding the fate of the Washington Post Company. She had no desire or intention to run the company. But as the new owner of the company, Graham had to either take the reins herself or give up control altogether. Though terrified by the prospect, Katharine Graham opted to take personal control of the company and accepted the job as its president.

It was a baptism by fire. In addition to knowing very little about running a newspaper, Graham also faced a company in which almost all positions of power were occupied by men. The idea that women were not capable of working for big business was as ingrained in Graham as it was in the *Post* employees. As a result, Graham ignored the quiet insults that came her way, because she privately agreed that as a woman she was simply not as qualified for the job as a man. Graham hired Ben Bradlee to become the new managing editor of *Washington Post*. Their partnership produced some of the greatest successes in the history of journalism.

In 1971 the *Post* obtained a copy of the Pentagon Papers, thousands of pages of previously secret information concerning the country's involvement in the war in Vietnam. Graham knew the *Post* would run serious legal risks if they chose to publish the information, but she did so. It was a watershed moment for freedom of the press and signaled the seriousness of the *Washington Post* in reporting news at any cost.

In 1972, following the break-in at the Democratic National Committee headquarters, a scandal now known as Watergate erupted. *Post* reporters Bob Woodward and Carl Bernstein ran an investigation of the scandal that revealed a massive government cover-up, ultimately resulting in the resignation of President Nixon himself.

In 1973, Katharine Graham became the chairman of the board and chief executive officer of the Post Company. That same year, the *Washington Post* won a Pulitzer Prize for its coverage of the Watergate scandal. By the mid-seventies, Graham was widely acknowledged as one of the most powerful women in the country. She knew and entertained many of the most influential political figures in

> "What I essentially did was to put one foot in front of the other, shut my eyes, and step off the edge. The surprise was that I landed on my feet."

Washington, including President Lyndon Johnson, Henry Kissinger, and President and Mrs. Reagan. She had come a long way from the soft-spoken self-described "doormat" housewife of the 1950s. When she published her autobiography in 1997, her self-told story won the Pulitzer Prize.

In the more than thirty years since Graham had reluctantly stepped up to fill her husband's shoes, she had transformed herself from an unassuming homemaker to the vastly influential head of a publishing empire. She disproved her own belief that women were not suited to business by leading the *Post* to a place on the Fortune 500 list as one the most profitable companies in the country. The world of journalism and the world of women remain indelibly marked by her life and accomplishments.

MARIA TALLCHIEF

First Native American prima ballerina

1925–

In 1925 on the Osage Indian Reservation in Oklahoma, a baby girl was born to Alexander Joseph Tall Chief and his wife, Ruth Porter Tall Chief. The girl, named Betty Marie Tall Chief, had her father's black hair and high cheekbones and her mother's love of dance and music. When Tall Chief turned three, her mother enrolled her in ballet class.

Tall Chief was an extremely good student, and her mother soon learned that the child also had perfect pitch, a relatively rare ability to hear any musical note and identify it correctly. Tall Chief began taking piano lessons as well, and her mother felt that she had the makings of a concert pianist. When she was not attending school, most of her day was filled with hours of ballet and piano practice. Tall Chief and her sister often performed at local events such as rodeos and county fairs. It was clear to Ruth Porter Tall Chief that both her daughters possessed unusual musical and dancing abilities. Believing it was vital that the girls obtain more advanced training, Tall Chief's mother convinced their father that the family should move to Los Angeles.

Ruth Porter Tall Chief learned that the famous ballerina Bronislava Nijinska was opening a teaching studio in the area. Nijinska and her brother, the world famous dancer Vaslav Nijinsky, were Russian dancers who had trained at the legendary Imperial Theatre School in St. Petersberg. The Russians represented the highest standard of ballet dancing in the world. Studying under Madame Nijinska, Tall Chief evolved into a potentially brilliant young protege.

When Nijinska decided to stage several of her own works at the Hollywood Bowl, she cast Tall Chief in a leading part. It was the first step toward becoming a professional ballet performer.

The head of the prestigious company Ballet Russe de Monte Carlo had seen Tall Chief dance during a visit to Madame Nijinska's school and had asked her to audition for him when she graduated from high school. Tall Chief traveled with an older dancer to New York City. Several days later, the 17-year-old had obtained an apprentice position with the Ballet Russe. She took the stage name Maria Tallchief, and her career began in earnest.

Tallchief embarked with the company on a tour of Canada and was given a full-time position with the company, at a salary of $40 a week. Though Tallchief was young and inexperienced, her spectacular talent was apparent to everyone. When one of the company's prima ballerinas argued with the director and quit, Tallchief found herself performing in the lead role of the ballet "Chopin Concerto" on opening night in New York City. She received solid reviews from critics for her work. Though she was relieved to return to a smaller role after several performances, Maria Tallchief had proven she could carry a performance in New York, in front of one of the country's most demanding audiences.

In 1943, the Russian choreographer George Balanchine was engaged by Ballet Russe to choreograph a program for the company. Within several years he and Tallchief established a legendary dancer/choreographer partnership. Tallchief ultimately married Balanchine, who would go on to be acknowledged as the greatest ballet choreographer of our time.

> "Because it was so unusual to see a Native American in ballet, I had to fight not to be exploited. I wanted to be recognized for my dancing and not solely because I was Osage."

Under Balanchine's close guidance, and dancing starring roles he created especially for her, Tallchief evolved from a gifted dancer to the country's most celebrated prima ballerina. Her performance in 1949's "Firebird," choreographed by Balanchine, confirmed her reputation as the most gifted ballerina our country had yet produced. She left Ballet Russe to join Balanchine's new company, the Ballet Society, which later became the New York City Ballet. When the couple's marriage dissolved in 1951, the working relationship between Tallchief and Balanchine endured. George Balanchine remained the primary influence on Tallchief's style and career until his death in 1983.

Tallchief received numerous prizes, such as the Capezio Dance Award. The State of Oklahoma honored her in 1953 with an Osage homecoming and gave her the name Princess Wa-XtheThonba, which translates as woman of two standards, or two worlds. She toured all over the globe and was invited to the White House to dance for President Eisenhower and later President Johnson. Tallchief continued performing until 1965. After she retired from performance, Tallchief continued to teach and give lectures, and she was asked to join the board of Americans for Indian Opportunity. In 1967, she was presented with the Indian Achievement Award by the Indian Council Fire. Married to her third husband, Buzz Paschen, Tallchief now spent more time at home in Chicago, raising her daughter, Elise. Nevertheless, she remained a key figure in the world of ballet, founding the Chicago Lyric Opera Ballet, which later became known as the Chicago City Ballet. After stepping down as the City Ballet's artistic director in 1987, Tallchief remained among the country's most visible and accomplished artists, receiving the Kennedy Center Honors in 1997 as one of the 20th century's outstanding artists and a National Medal of the Arts and Humanities from President Clinton in 1999. Her achievements in the world of ballet are still considered among the greatest, and her legend will certainly never be surpassed.

QUOTE SOURCES

In most cases, check the Bibliography for the full citation of a source.

Wilma Mankiller: *Mankiller, A Chief and Her People*, p. 112.

Elizabeth Blackwell: *Pioneer Work in Opening the Medical Profession to Women*, p. 174 (journal excerpt 2 Sept. 1849).

Wilma Rudolph: *Wilma: The Story of Wilma Rudolph*, p. 65.

Victoria Murden: "Letters from the Edge," 21 Sept. 1999.

Margaret Bourke-White: *Portrait of Myself*, p. 90.

Susan Butcher: Interview by the Hall of Sports.

Jane Addams: "The Working Woman's Need of the Ballot," by Jane Addams, *Women's Journal*, 27 Nov. 1897.

Madam C. J. Walker: *On Her Own Ground: The Life and Times of Madam C. J. Walker*, p. 68.

Nellie Bly: *Nellie Bly: Daredevil, Reporter, Feminist*, p. 85.

Emma Hart Willard: *Mrs. Willard's Plan of Female Education*, p. 12.

Lynn Hill: Interview by Kathleen Gasperini.

Phillis Wheatley: "On the Death of General Wooster," *Complete Writings*, p. 93.

Stacy Allison: *Beyond the Limits: A Woman's Triumph on Everest*, p. 282.

Marian Anderson: *My Lord, What a Morning*, p. 309.

Kathrine Switzer: "Sports Women; Marathon's Pioneers Made Great Strides."

Frances Perkins: *Frances Perkins: Champion of the New Deal*, p. 73.

Harriet Quimby: "How I Won My Aviator's License—Part Three."

Pearl S. Buck: *Of Men and Women*, by Pearl S. Buck. New York: John Day, 1941, p. 20.

Olga Samaroff Stokowski: *An American Musician's Story*, by Olga Samaroff Stokowski. New York: W.W. Norton, 1939, p. 179.

Carrie Chapman Catt: Early speech, *Charles City Ingelligencer*, 28 June 1877, p. 2.

Shirley Muldowney: "Shirley Muldowney." *Contemporary Newsmakers*.

Sally Priesand: "Celebrating 30 Years of Women as Rabbis."

Julia Morgan: *Julia Morgan: Architect of Dreams*, p. 121.

Gertrude Ederle: "'It Had to Be Done, I Did It.'"

Jane Roberts: *Dreams, Evolution, and Value Fulfillment*, by Jane Roberts. New York: Prentice Hall Press, 1986. Vol. 1, p. 183.

Georgia O'Keeffe: *Portrait of an Artist: A Biography of Georgia O'Keeffe*, p. 173.

Kathleen McGrath: "Aye Aye, Ma'am."

Fanny Bullock Workman: *On Top of the World: Five Women Explorers in Tibet*, p. 128.

Eve Queler: "All About Eve—One of the Nation's Few Women Conductors Overcomes Prejudice to Build Music Career."

Rita Dove: Online interview by M. Wynn Thomas.

Helen Keller: *The Story of My Life*, p. 99.

Antonia Novello: "Antonia Novello: A Dream Come True."

Brenda Berkman: Interview by Amy Gage.

Laura Ingalls Wilder: "The Making of Little House on the Prairie," p. 287.

Dian Fossey: *Woman in the Mists*, p. 365.

Sacagawea: Quote by William Clark, journal entry dated 13 Oct. 1805. http://www.infoplease.com/t/hist/lewis-clark-journal/day518.html.

Edna St. Vincent Millay: "First Fig," *The Norton Anthology of Modern Poetry*. New York: W.W. Norton, 2nd ed., 1988, p. 525.

Martha Graham: *Martha: The Life and Work of Martha Graham*, p. 373.

Katharine Graham: *Personal History*, p. 341.

Maria Tallchief: "En Pointe, Center Stage," by Jason Ryle, *National Museum of the American Indian*, winter 2003, p. 2.

SELECTED BIBLIOGRAPHY

WILMA MANKILLER

"Chief Wilma Mankiller Helps Cherokees Build Pride." *U.S. News & World Report*, 17 Feb. 1986, p. 64.

Holloway, Sue. "Indigenous Wisdom: Cherokee Chief Thrives in Contemporary World." *Fairfield County Woman*, 31 Dec. 1998, p. 12.

Mankiller, Wilma. *Mankiller, A Chief and Her People.* New York: St. Martin's Press, 1993.

ELIZABETH BLACKWELL

Blackwell, Elizabeth. *Pioneer Work in Opening the Medical Profession to Women.* Penzance: British Heritage Database, 2003. First edition published 1895.

Glimm, Adele. *Elizabeth Blackwell: First Woman Doctor of Modern Times.* New York: McGraw Hill, 2000.

Kline, Nancy. *Elizabeth Blackwell: A Doctor's Triumph.* Berkeley: Conari Press, 1997.

WILMA RUDOLPH

Biracree, Tom. *Wilma Rudolph: Champion Athlete.* Philadelphia: Chelsea House Publishers, 1988.

Litsky, Frank. "Wilma Rudolph, Star of the 1960 Oympics, Dies at 54." *New York Times*, 13 Nov. 1994, p. 53.

Rudolph, Wilma. *Wilma: The Story of Wilma Rudolph.* New York: New American Library, 1977.

VICTORIA MURDEN

Cameron, Gail. "The Unsinkable Tori Murden." *Smith Alumnae Quarterly*, fall 2000, pp. 14–23.

Murden, Victoria. "Letters from the Edge." www.adept.net/americanpearl. 4 Sept. 1999– 29 Nov. 1999.

Stahl, Linda. "Louisville Rower Conquers Atlantic." *Louisville Courier-Journal*, 4 Dec. 1999, p. 1, p. 7.

MARGARET BOURKE-WHITE

Bourke-White, Margaret. *Portrait of Myself.* New York: Simon and Schuster, 1963.

Rubin, Susan Goldman. *Margaret Bourke-White: Her Pictures Were Her Life.* New York: Harry N. Abrams, 1999.

Welch, Catherine A. *Margaret Bourke-White: Racing with a Dream.* Minneapolis: Carolrhoda Books, 1998.

SUSAN BUTCHER

Butcher, Susan. Interview by the Hall of Sports. www.achievement.org. 29 June 1991.

Dolan, Ellen M. *Susan Butcher and the Iditarod Trail.* New York: Walker, 1993.

Lloyd, Barbara. "Iditarod's Icy Odyssey Is Butcher's Highway." *New York Times,* 6 March 1994, p. S4.

JANE ADDAMS

Davis, Allen F. *American Heroine: The Life and Legend of Jane Addams.* Chicago: Ivan R. Dee, 2000.

"Jane Addams." www.spartacus.schoolnet.co.uk/USAaddams.htm.

"Jane Addams—Biography." Nobel e-Museum. www.nobel.se/peace/laureates/1931/addams-bio.html.

MADAM C. J. WALKER

Brown, Mitchell C. "The Faces of Science: African Americans in the Sciences." www.princeton.edu/~mcbrown. June 2000.

Bundles, A'Lelia. *On Her Own Ground: The Life and Times of Madam C. J. Walker.* New York: Washington Square Press, 2001.

NELLIE BLY

Fredeen, Charles. *Nellie Bly: Daredevil Reporter.* Minneapolis: Lerner Publications, 2000.

Kroeger, Brooke. *Nellie Bly: Daredevil, Reporter, Feminist.* New York: Times Books, 1994.

Marks, Jason. *Around the World in 72 Days: The Race Between Pulitzer's Nellie Bly & Cosmopolitan's Elizabeth Bisland.* Pittsburgh: Sterling House, 1999.

EMMA HART WILLARD

Lutz, Alma. *Emma Willard: Daughter of Democracy.* Cambridge: Riverside Press, 1929.

Scott, Anne Firor. "What, Then, Is the American: This New Woman?" *Journal of American History,* Vol. 45, No. 3, Dec. 1978, pp. 679–703.

Willard, Emma Hart. *Mrs. Willard's Plan of Female Education: An Address to the Public: Particularly to the Members of the Legislature of New York.* 1819 edition. Emma Willard School Archives, Troy, New York.

LYNN HILL

Hill, Lynn. "El Capitan's Nose Climbed Free." *American Alpine Journal*, 1994, pp. 41-49.

Hill, Lynn. Interview by Kathleen Gasperini. "Going to Extremes with Lynn Hill and Nancy Feagin." http://classic.mountainzone.com/climbing/hill.

Hill, Lynn. Interview with *Outside Magazine*. July 1996. www.outsidemag.com/disc/guest/hill/profile.html.

Hill, Lynn, with Greg Child. *Climbing Free: My Life in the Vertical World*. New York: W. W. Norton, 2002.

PHILLIS WHEATLEY

"Historic Figures: Phillis Wheatley." www.bbc.co.uk/history/historic_figures/wheatley_phillis.shtml.

Salisbury, Cynthia. *Phillis Wheatley: Legendary African-American Poet*. Berkeley Heights: Enslow Publishers, 2001.

Wheatley, Phillis. *Complete Writings*. New York: Penguin Books, 2001.

STACY ALLISON

Allison, Stacy, with Peter Carlin. *Beyond the Limits: A Woman's Triumph on Everest*. Boston: Little, Brown, 1993.

Coburn, Broughton. *Everest: Mountain Without Mercy*. Washington: National Geographic Society, 1997.

Couzens, Gerald Secor. "To the Roof of the World." *Newsday*, 21 April 1990, Part 2, p. 7.

MARIAN ANDERSON

Anderson, Marian. *My Lord, What a Morning*. Illinois: University of Illinois Press, 1956, and 2002.

"Remembering Marian Anderson." Online NewsHour transcript. www.pbs.org/newshour/bb/remember/1997/anderson_2-26a.html.

KATHRINE SWITZER

Bynum, Chris. "Running Revolutionary." *Times-Picayune*, 4 Oct. 2001, "Living," p. 1.

Matson, Barbara. "Sports Women: Marathon's Pioneers Made Great Strides—These Women Refused to Be Banned in Boston." *Boston Globe*, 10 April 2002, F10.

O'Farrell, Peggy. "Cultivating a Will to Run: Marathon Pioneer Kathrine Switzer Urges Women to Take the First Step Toward Exercise." *Cincinnati Enquirer*, 19 Sept. 2000. http://enquirer.com/editions/2000/09/19/loc_cultivating_will_to.html.

Stiehm, Jamie. "Runners' Stories Target Self-Esteem." *Baltimore Sun*, 24 April 1999. www.baltimoresun.com/search/.

Switzer, Kathrine. *Running and Walking for Women over 40*. New York: St. Martin's Press, 1998.

FRANCES PERKINS

Berg, Gordon. " 'Be Ye Steadfast': The Life and Work of Frances Perkins." U.S. Department of Labor, www.dol.gov/opa/frances/frances.htm.

Pasachoff, Naomi. *Francis Perkins: Champion of the New Deal*. New York: Oxford University Press, 1999.

HARRIET QUIMBY

"Chasing the Sun: Harriet Quimby." www.pbs.org/kcet/chasingthesun/innovators/hquimby.html.

Hall, Ed. Y. *Harriet Quimby: America's First Lady of the Air*. Spartanburg: Honoribus Press, 1990.

Quimby, Harriet. "The Dangers of Flying and How to Avoid Them." *Leslie's Illustrated Weekly*, 31 Aug. 1911.

Quimby, Harriet. "How I Won My Aviator's License—Part Three." *Leslie's Illustrated Weekly*, 24 Aug. 1911.

PEARL S. BUCK

Conn, Peter. *Pearl S. Buck: A Cultural Biography*. Cambridge: Cambridge University Press, 1996.

Pearl S. Buck International. "About Our Founder." www.pearl-s-buck.org/psbi/PearlSBuck/about.asp.

OLGA SAMAROFF STOKOWSKI

Kline, Donna Staley. *Olga Samaroff Stokowski: An American Virtuoso on the World Stage*. College Station: Texas A&M University Press, 1996.

"Leopold Stokowski: Making Music Matter." Penn Library Exhibitions. www.library.upenn.edu/special/gallery/stokowski.

McGillen, Geoffrey E. "Olga Samaroff." *The Handbook of Texas Online*. www.tsha.utexas.edu/handbook/online/articles/view/SS/fsa47.html.

CARRIE CHAPMAN CATT

Van Voris, Jacqueline. *Carrie Chapman Catt: A Public Life*. New York. Feminist Press at the City University of New York, 1987.

"Women's Suffrage." Microsoft Encarta Encyclopedia, 1993–1998, Microsoft Corporation.

SHIRLEY MULDOWNEY

"Despite a 250 MPH Crash and Six Operations, This Lady Can't Wait to Prove She's Still a Champ." *People Magazine*, 16 Sept. 1985, p. 143.

"A Lifetime of Devotion" www.muldowney.com/devotion/htm.

Muldowney, Shirley. *Shirley Muldowney's Tales from the Track*. Champaign, Ill. Sports Publishing, 2005.

"Shirley Muldowney." *Contemporary Newsmakers*. Gale Research, 1987.

SALLY PRIESAND

Blau, Eleanor. "1st Woman Rabbi in U.S. Ordained." *New York Times*, 4 June, 1972, p. 76.

Mendelsohn, Martha. "First Lady of the Rabbinate: Twenty-five Years After Becoming the First-ever Woman Rabbi, Sally Priesand Is Still Committed to Empowerment." *Jewish Week*, 12 Sept. 1997, p. 16.

Nadell, Pamela S. *Women Who Would Be Rabbis*. Boston: Beacon Press, 1998.

Priesand, Sally. "Celebrating 30 Years of Women as Rabbis." Kolel Adult Centre for Liberal Jewish Learning. www.kolel.org/pages/priesand.html.

Shear, Jeffrey. "Woman Rabbi Sees 'A Long Way to Go.'" *New York Times*, 9 Dec. 1979, p. NJ22.

JULIA MORGAN

Boutelle, Sandra Holmes, and Richard Barnes. *Julia Morgan, Architect*. New York, Abbeville Press, 1995.

"Julia's Story." Julia Morgan Center for the Arts. www.juliamorgan.org/story.html.

"The Julia Morgan Collection." Special Collections, California Polytechnic University, Robert E. Kennedy Library. www.lib.calpoly.edu/spec_coll/morgan/bio/bio.html.

Wadsworth, Ginger. *Julia Morgan, Architect of Dreams*. Minneapolis: Lerner Publications, 1990.

GERTRUDE EDERLE

Anderson, Kelli. "The Young Woman and the Sea: August 6, 1926 Gertrude Ederle Crosses the English Channel." *Sports Illustrated*, 29 Nov. 1999, p. 90.

Bock, Hal. "Ederle's Anniversary: Swimming the English Channel." Associated Press, 4 Aug. 2001.

Maeder, Jay. "Swim It or Drown: Gertrude of America, 1926." *Daily News*, 26 April 1998, p. 39.

Rutherford, Alec. "'It Had to Be Done, I Did It,' Says Miss Ederle." *New York Times*, 7 Aug. 1926, p. 1.

Severo, Richard. "Gertrude Ederle, the First Woman to Swim Across the English Channel, Dies at 98." *New York Times*, 1 Dec. 2003.

JANE ROBERTS

Roberts, Jane. *The Nature of Personal Beauty*. Englewood Cliffs: Prentice-Hall Books, 1974.

Roberts, Jane. *Seth Speaks*. Englewood Cliffs: Prentice-Hall Books, 1972.

Watkins, Susan M. *Speaking of Jane Roberts: Remembering the Author of the Seth Material*. Portsmouth: Moment Point Press, 2001.

GEORGIA O'KEEFFE

Asbury, Edith Evans. "Georgia O'Keeffe Dead at 90: Shaper of Modern Art in U.S." *New York Times*, 7 March 1986, p. 1.

Costantino, Maria. *Georgia O' Keeffe*. New York: Smithmark Publishers, 1995.

Drohojowska, Hunter. "Art O'Keeffe: Georgia on His Mind: An Exhibit at Getty Museum Casts New Light on the Relationship Between Artist Georgia O'Keeffe and Photographer Alfred Stieglitz." *Los Angeles Times*, 28 June 1992, p. 78.

Hogrefe, Jeffrey. *O'Keeffe: The Life of an American Legend*. New York: Bantam Books, 1992.

Lisle, Laurie. *Portrait of an Artist: A Biography of Georgia O'Keeffe*. New York: Washington Square Press, 1980 and 1986.

KATHLEEN MCGRATH

Brooks, Clark. "Spouse, Kids Wave Adieu to Captain and Her Warship." *San Diego Union Tribune*, 1 April 2000, p. B-27.

Brown, Justin. "A Crack Appears on the Navy's Brass Ceiling." *Christian Science Monitor*, 31 March 2000, p. 1.

"Kathleen McGrath, Warship Captain, Died on September 26th, Age 50." *Economist*, 3 Oct. 2002. http://www.economist.com/people/displayStory.cfm?story_id=1365052.

Thompson, Mark. "Aye Aye, Ma'am: The Navy Makes History as It Sends the First U.S. Warship Ever Commanded by a Woman Toward the Troubled Waters of the Persian Gulf." *Time Magazine*, 27 March 2000, p. 30.

Watson, Molly. "America's First Woman-of-War." *Evening Standard* (London), 27 March 2000.

Woo, Elaine. "Kathleen McGrath, 50; 1st Woman to Command a U.S. Navy Warship." *Los Angeles Times*, 3 Oct. 2002. www.latimes.com/news/printedition/california/la-me-mcgrath3oct03.story.

FANNY BULLOCK WORKMAN

Mazel, David, ed. *Mountaineering Woman: Stories by Early Climbers*. College Station: Texas A&M Press, 1994.

Miller, Luree. *On Top of the World: Five Women Explorers in Tibet*. Seattle: Mountaineers, 1984.

Scully, Lizzy. "In the Footsteps of Fanny: Women in the Karakoram." *Climbing Magazine*, June 2003. http://climbing.com/current/wmnkarakrm/.

EVE QUELER

Crean, Elisabeth A. "Conducting Life with Passion: From a 'Shy' Opera Conductor Come Eloquent Stories." *Honolulu Star-Bulletin*, 20 March 1997. http://starbulletin.com/97/03/20/features/story3.html.

Kline, Betsy. "They Conduct Themselves Well in a Highly Competitive Field." *Pittsburgh Post Gazette*, 12 June 1994, p. H1.

Kors, Stacy. "All About Eve: Eve Queler's Opera Orchestra Turns 25." *American Record Guide*, March 1996, p. 25.

Krauss, Melvyn. "All About Eve—Eve Queler and the Opera Orchestra of New York." *World and I*, p. 78.

Midgette, Anne. "The Wisdom of Eve." *Opera News*, Vol. 64, No. 4, 1 Oct. 1999, p. 48.

Winship, Frederick M. "All About Eve—One of the Nation's Few Women Conductors Overcomes Prejudice to Build Music Career." UPI, 1 May 1982.

RITA DOVE

"Comprehensive Biography of Rita Dove." The Rita Dove Home Page. www.people.virginia.edu/~rfd4b/compbio.html.

Dove, Rita. Online interview by M. Wynn Thomas. www.english.uiuc.edu/maps/poets/a_f/dove/mwthomas.htm. 12 Aug. 1995.

Dove, Rita. *The Poet's World*. Washington: Library of Congress, 1995.

Dove, Rita. *Selected Poems*. New York: Vintage Books, 1993.

HELEN KELLER

Hermann, Dorothy. *Helen Keller: A Life*. New York: Alfred A. Knopf, 1998.

Keller, Helen. *Light in My Darkness*. 2nd ed. West Chester, Penn.: Chrysalis Books, 2000.

Keller, Helen. *The Story of My Life*. New York: Bantam Books, 1990.

Lash, Joseph P. *Helen and Teacher: The Story of Helen Keller and Anne Sullivan Macy*. New York: Delacorte Press/Seymour Lawrence, 1980.

ANTONIA NOVELLO

Hawxhurst, Joan C. *Antonia Novello: U.S. Surgeon General*. Brookfield, Conn.: Millbrook Press, 1993.

Hilts, Philip J. "President Picks Hispanic Woman to Become U.S. Surgeon General." *New York Times*, 18 Oct. 1989, p. A20.

Krucoff, Carol. "Antonia Novello: A Dream Come True: United States Surgeon General." *Saturday Evening Post*, May 1991, p. 38.

Stoltz, Craig. "Just Say Novello." *ADWEEK*, 18 Nov. 1991, section dossier d.c.

BRENDA BERKMAN

Berkman, Brenda. Interview by Amy Gage. *St. Olaf College News*, May 2002. http://www.stolaf.edu/news/interview/berkman/.

Berkman, Brenda. Interview by Elizabeth Kimmel. May 2003.

Hagen, Susan, and Mary Carouba. *Women at Ground Zero*. Indianapolis: Alpha Books, 2002.

Haller, Vera. "For Woman Firefighter, a Job She Loves." *Newsday*, 14 March 2002.

Shenon, Philip. "2 Women Win Bias Suit Against Fire Dept." *New York Times*, 9 Dec. 1983, p. A1.

Stabiner, Karen. "The Storm over Women Firefighters." *New York Times Magazine*, 26 Sept. 1982, p. 100.

LAURA INGALLS WILDER

Anderson, William. *Laura Ingalls Wilder: A Biography*. New York: HarperTrophy, 1992.

Anderson, William. "The Making of Little House on the Prairie: A 65th Anniversary Retrospective." *Little House on the Prairie: Collector's Edition*. New York: HarperCollins, 1999.

Collins, Carolyn Strom, and Christina Wyss Erksson. *Inside Laura's Little House: The Little House on the Prairie Treasury*. New York: HarperCollins, 2000.

Collins, Carolyn Strom, and Christina Wyss Eriksson. *The World of Little House*. New York: HarperCollins, 1996.

Zochert, Donald. *Laura: The Life of Laura Ingalls Wilder, Author of The Little House on the Prairie*. New York: Avon Books, 1976.

DIAN FOSSEY

Fawcett, Katie. "Virunga Gorilla Census Shows 17% Increase." *The Dian Fossey Gorilla Journal*, Winter 2004, p. 1.

Fossey, Dian. *Gorillas in the Mist*. Boston: Houghton Mifflin, 1983.

"Karisoke Research Center." www.gorillafund.org.

Mowat, Farley. *Woman in the Mists: the Story of Dian Fossey and the Mountain Gorillas of Africa*. New York: Warner Books, 1987.

SACAGAWEA

Ambrose, Stephen E. *Undaunted Courage: Meriwether Lewis, Thomas Jefferson, and the Opening of the American West*. New York: Touchstone Books, 1996.

DeVoto, Bernard, ed. *The Journals of Lewis and Clark*. Boston: Mariner Books, 1997.

Hunsaker, Joyce Badgley. "Who Was Sacagawea?" *Time Magazine*, 8 July 2002. http://www.time.com/time/2002/lewis_clark/lsacagawea/html.

Schmidt, Thomas, and Jeremy Schmidt. *The Saga of Lewis & Clark: Into the Uncharted West*. New York: DK Publishing, 1999.

EDNA ST. VINCENT MILLAY

Ellmann, Richard, and Robert O'Clair, eds. *The Norton Anthology of Modern Poetry*, 2nd ed. New York: W. W. Norton, 1988.

Gale, Robert L. "Edna St. Vincent Millay's Life." American National Biography Online. www.anb.org/articles/16/16-01131.html.

Milford, Nancy. *Savage Beauty: The Life of Edna St. Vincent Millay*. New York: Random House, 2001.

MARTHA GRAHAM

DeMille, Agnes. *Martha: The Life and Work of Martha Graham*. New York: Random House, 1991.

Freedman, Russell. *Martha Graham: A Dancer's Life*. New York: Clarion Books, 1998.

Tracy, Robert. *Goddess: Martha Graham's Dancers Remember*. New York: Limelight, 1997.

KATHARINE GRAHAM

Graham, Katharine. *Personal History*. New York: Vintage Books, 1997.

Reaves, Jessica. "Katharine Graham: 1917–2001; The Woman Who Took Over a Publishing Empire and Led Woodward, Bernstein and Bradlee Through Watergate Is Dead at 84." *Time Magazine*, 17 July 2001.
http://www.time.com/time/nation/article/0,8599,167941,00.html.

Smith, H. Y., and Noel Epstein. "Katharine Graham Dies at 84: She Guided Post Through Pentagon Papers and Watergate to Fortune 500." *Washington Post*, 18 July 2001, p. A1.

MARIA TALLCHIEF

Gourley, Catherine. *Who Is Maria Tallchief?* New York: Grosset & Dunlap, 2002.

Ryle, Jason. "En Pointe, Center Stage." *National Museum of the American Indian*, winter 2003, p. 2.

Tallchief, Maria, with Larry Kaplan. *America's Prima Ballerina*. New York: Henry Holt, 1997.

CHRONOLOGY

1767

Phillis Wheatley's work (a poem) is published for the first time in a newspaper, making her the first African American woman writer to be published.

1806

Sacagawea becomes the first Native American woman accorded the right to vote in an official U.S. government venture when given an equal vote as a member of the Corps of Discovery.

1821

Emma Hart Willard's hard work promoting higher education for women results in the opening of Troy Female Seminary, the first higher education institution for women.

1845

Elizabeth Blackwell is admitted to Geneva Medical College of Western New York. She completes her course of study and becomes the first American woman to graduate from medical school.

January 25, 1890

Nelly Bly becomes the first woman to travel around the world in under 80 days.

1900

Helen Keller graduates from the prestigious Radcliffe College. She is the first blind and deaf woman to graduate from college.

1900

Julia Morgan becomes the first American woman admitted to the Ecoles des Beaux-Arts Architecture School.

January 18, 1905

Olga Samaroff Stokowski becomes the first American woman to debut at Carnegie Hall.

1906-1919

Madame C. J. Walker develops her own hair care products for African American women and becomes the first female African American self-made millionaire.

1906

At the age of 47, Fanny Bullock Workman becomes the first woman to summit Pinnacle Peak in Kashmir.

1911

Harriet Quimby becomes the first American woman and the second woman in the world to obtain a license to fly.

1920

Carrie Chapman Catt becomes the first woman to call for a league of women voters. The League of Women Voters was founded during the convention of the National American Woman Suffrage Association.

1923

Edna St. Vincent Millay becomes the first woman awarded the Pulitzer Prize for Poetry, for her work *The Ballad of the Harp-Weaver: A Few Figs from Thistles: Eight Sonnets in American Poetry*.

August 6, 1926

Nineteen-year-old Gertrude Ederle becomes the first woman to swim across the English Channel, swimming a total of 35 miles.

1931

Jane Addams becomes the first American woman to win the Nobel Peace Prize and is honored for her ideals and peacekeeping efforts.

1931

Martha Graham becomes the first dancer to win a Guggenheim Fellowship, a prestigious award enabling her to more easily pursue her art.

1933

Frances Perkins becomes Secretary of Labor for the Roosevelt administration and the first woman to hold a cabinet position in the United States Government.

1933-1949

Maria Tallchief becomes an accomplished dancer and the first Native American prima ballerina.

1938

Pearl S. Buck, a Pulitzer Prize winning author, becomes the first American woman to win the Nobel Prize for literature.

1941

Margaret Bourke-White is given permission to travel with a B-17 bomber to Africa to photograph combat. She becomes the first woman photographer to document active war combat missions.

1946

Georgia O'Keeffe becomes the first woman given a Retrospective Exhibit by New York's Museum of Modern Art.

1954

Marian Anderson becomes the first African American woman to sing with the Metropolitan Opera. Her first performance was *The Masked Ball*.

1954

Laura Ingalls Wilder becomes the first writer to win the American Library Association's Laura Ingalls Wilder Medal for Substantial Contribution to Children's Literature.

1960

Wilma Rudolph qualifies for the Olympic team and travels to Rome. She wins her first Olympic gold medal in the 100-meter dash, her second Olympic gold medal in the 200-meter dash, and her third Olympic gold medal in the 400-meter relay. She becomes the first American woman to win three gold medals at a single Olympics.

1960s

Eve Queler becomes the first American woman to conduct at a major European Opera House, appearing in Nice, Barcelona, and at the Frankfurt Opera.

1963

Katharine Graham becomes the first woman to head a Fortune 500 company when she becomes president of the *Washington Post* Company after the death of her husband.

1963

Jane Roberts becomes the first author of a multi-volume metaphysical work whose writing is included in the Yale Archives.

1966

Dian Fossey becomes the first woman zoologist to study mountain gorillas in their habitat.

1967

Kathrine Switzer becomes the first woman to officially enter and run the Boston Marathon at a time when women were not allowed to enter marathons. Her entrance and completion of the race sparked an outcry, and in 1971 the rules were changed to include women.

June 3, 1972

Sally Priesand becomes the first American woman ordained as a rabbi.

1982-1983

Brenda Berkman becomes the first woman to challenge the ban on women in the Fire Department of the City of New York. She becomes a firefighter, and today she is a captain.

1985

After the incumbent chief assumes a new position, Wilma Mankiller becomes principal chief of the Cherokee Nation and the first woman to hold the position. She remains chief until 1995.

1986

Susan Butcher wins her first Iditarod, which takes 11 days.

1987

Butcher wins her second Iditarod and beats her old record.

1988

Butcher wins her third Iditarod and becomes the first person ever to win three consecutive races.

1988

Stacy Allison becomes the first American woman to summit Mount Everest.

1989

Antonia Novello is nominated by President George Bush and becomes the first woman and Hispanic Surgeon General of the United States.

1993

Rita Dove, a Pulitzer Prize winning poet, becomes the Poet Laureate of the United States. She is the first African American and the youngest person to hold this position.

1993

Lynn Hill becomes the first person to perform a free rock-climbing ascent of the Nose at Yosemite. She completes the climb in a record four days. The following year she shocks fellow climbers by completing the same free-climb in just 23 hours.

1998

Kathleen McGrath becomes the first woman to command a U.S. Navy warship, the U.S.S. *Jarrett*.

December 3, 1999

Victoria Murden arrives in Guadeloupe, successfully finishing her solo row across the Atlantic Ocean. She becomes the first woman to row across the Atlantic.

2004

After a long racing career and many distinguished awards, Shirley Muldowney becomes the first woman to be inducted into the Motorsports Hall of Fame.

INDEX